The Book
of Jewish
Holidays

The Book

Illustrated by SUSANNE SUBA

# of Jewish Holidays

RUTH KOZODOY

BEHRMAN HOUSE, INC.
Publishers & Booksellers

For SARAH, PETER, and ELIZABETH

Acknowledgements

I thank the following people who helped prepare this book for publication: Rabbi Daniel Teplitz, for his constructive advice on the book's organization; Rahel Bloch and Rabbi Morrison D. Bial, for substantive suggestions; Susanne Suba for her beautiful art; Seymour Rossel, who edited the manuscript and Karen Rossel, the copy editor.

I especially thank Neal Kozodoy for the inspiration, encouragement, and invaluable counsel he gave throughout.   R.K.

PHOTO CREDITS

LENI SONNENFELD, New York, N.Y.
Pages 10, 12, 19, 29, 32, 39, 41, 45, 53, 70, 74, 76 (top), 84, 85, 87, 128 (lower left), 134, 142, 144, 147 (bottom), 157, 162 (bottom), 170 (lower right).
BILL ARON, Los Angeles, California
14, 34 (right), 40, 54, 58 (top), 61, 76 (bottom), 106, 120, 127, 128 (bottom right), 130, 147 (top, center)
RICHARD NOWITZ, Jerusalem   28, 34 (left), 119, 128 (top).
THE JEWISH MUSEUM, N.Y.   15, 55, 58 (bottom), 75 (top right), 78, 79, 107 (left), 114 (bottom right), 152, 153
RELIGIOUS NEWS SERVICE PHOTOS, New York   114 (bottom left), 176 (bottom), 185.
ISRAEL CONSULATE GENERAL LIBRARY, New York   24, 35, 96, 114 (top), 128 (center left and right), 136, 158, 183
ZIONIST ARCHIVES AND LIBRARY, NEW YORK   170 (top), 170 (lower left), 176 (top), 179.
CENTRAL CONFERENCE OF AMERICAN RABBIS   75 (upper left).
NATIONAL AERONAUTICS AND SPACE ADM.   189.

Library of Congress Cataloging in Publication Data

Kozodoy, Ruth.
    The book of Jewish holidays.

    Summary: Discusses the significance and the customs of various Jewish holidays including Sukkot, Purim, and Yom Hashoah.

    1. Fasts and feasts—Judaism—Juvenile literature. [1. Fasts and feasts—Judaism]
I. Title.
BM690.K65   296.4'3   81-9970
ISBN 0-87441-334-6   AACR2

Project Editor: RALPH DAVIS

Published by Behrman House, Inc.
235 Watchung Avenue
West Orange, NJ 07052

MANUFACTURED IN THE
UNITED STATES OF AMERICA

CONTENTS

A CHART OF THE JEWISH YEAR

The Seasons	The Months	The Holidays	
FALL סְתָו	Tishre תִּשְׁרֵי	Rosh Hashanah רֹאשׁ הַשָּׁנָה	1-2
		Yom Kippur יוֹם כִּפּוּר	10
		Sukkot סֻכּוֹת	15-22
		Simhat Torah שִׂמְחַת תּוֹרָה	23
	Heshvan חֶשְׁוָן also called, Marheshvan מַרְחֶשְׁוָן		
	Kislev כִּסְלֵו	Hanukkah חֲנֻכָּה	25 Kislev- 2 Tevet
WINTER חֹרֶף	Tevet טֵבֵת		
	Shevat שְׁבָט	Tu bi-Shevat ט״ו בִּשְׁבָט	15
	Adar אֲדָר	Purim (in a leap year, פּוּרִים in Adar Sheni)	14
	Adar Sheni אֲדָר שֵׁנִי (extra month, added in leap years)		
SPRING אָבִיב	Nisan נִיסָן	Pesah פֶּסַח	15-22
		Yom Hashoah יוֹם הַשּׁוֹאָה	27
	Iyar אִיָּר	Yom Hazikkaron יוֹם הַזִּכָּרוֹן	4
		Yom Ha'atzma'ut יוֹם הָעַצְמָאוּת	5
		Lag ba-Omer לַ״ג בָּעֹמֶר	18
		Yom Yerushalayim יוֹם יְרוּשָׁלַיִם	28
	Sivan סִיוָן	Shavuot שָׁבוּעוֹת	6-7
SUMMER קַיִץ	Tammuz תַּמּוּז		
	Av אָב	Tisha be-Av תִּשְׁעָה בְּאָב	9
	Elul אֱלוּל		

The Bible and Jewish holidays

The most important Jewish holidays are the ones mentioned in the Torah. These are our oldest holidays. They are commanded by God.

The biblical holidays are the High Holy Days; Shabbat; and the three pilgrimage festivals (*Shalosh Regalim*)—Sukkot, Pesah, and Shavuot. During the three pilgrimage festivals, in ancient times, Jews travelled from their homes to Jerusalem, to make offerings in the Temple to God.

When we observe these biblical holidays, we are celebrating the same events—and sometimes, in exactly the same way—that our ancestors did, thousands of years ago.

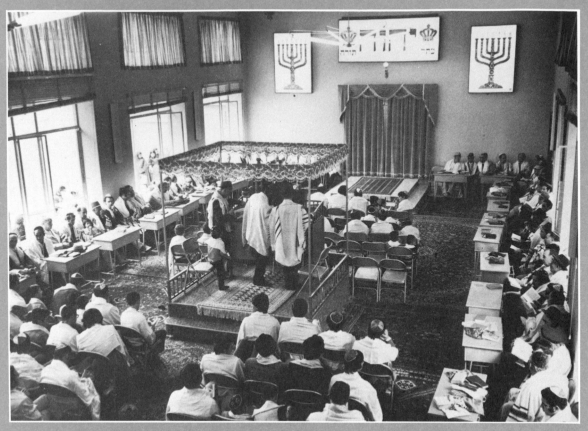

This Rosh Hashanah service is being celebrated in Israel by Sephardic (Spanish) Jews. It is a Sephardic custom to place the altar in the center of the synagogue.

Beginning
A Sweet
New Year

Rosh Hashanah

A Sweet New Year Begins

The summer has ended. New things begin: a new class in school, new work, new adventures, new friends. And another, most important thing—a new year. Now, according to our Jewish calendar, comes *Rosh Hashanah*, the "head"—the beginning—of the year.

When a new year comes, it makes us think. We think about the year ahead: what we plan to do, how we hope our lives will be. This changing of one year into the next is important. We want to get ready for it. We are happy and excited, our heads are filled with a dizzying number of thoughts.

LESHANAH TOVAH   *Sending Rosh Hashanah cards is a custom that goes back many years. These cards are more than sixty years old. The box in the card on the left contains a New Year's poem in Yiddish.*

LOOKING FORWARD, LOOKING BACK

One way we celebrate Rosh Hashanah is by looking forward. We dip slices of apple or *ḥallah* into honey, and eat them, saying, "May it be a sweet and good year." We send Rosh Hashanah cards. Rosh Hashanah is, in a way, a celebration of the world's creation, the "birthday" of the world. So we wish the world, and each other, a happy year ahead.

Also, we remember the last new year. It seems that a whole year has slipped by very quickly. Now we look back; we remember. In fact, "Day of Remembering" is the

On Rosh Hashanah eve we greet each other with a special greeting, *Leshanah Tovah Tikatevu*. It means, "May God write you down for a good year." There is an old legend that God keeps a great book containing everyone's name, and during the High Holy Days He writes down, in this Book of Life, whether or not each person has led a good life during the year. This is just a legend, of course. It shows that Rosh Hashanah is a day when our actions are judged by God and by ourselves. Another name for Rosh Hashanah is *Yom Hadin*, Day of Judgment.

name the Torah gives to Rosh Hashanah. We remember because what has *already* happened tells us something about what *will* happen. If we want to be proud of ourselves in the year ahead, we must think about how we have done so far.

And so, on Rosh Hashanah, we think over our lives. We promise ourselves to do our very best in the future. Doing that helps us feel clean and strong, and fills us with energy for new things.

On the eve of Rosh Hashanah we celebrate with a delicious holiday dinner. We have a special ḥallah that is round, like the crown of a king or queen. That's because on Rosh Hashanah we think of God as a kind, loving King.

Rosh Hashanah in the Synagogue

For the Rosh Hashanah services, we go to the synagogue. The curtains of the Ark and the Torah covers are beautiful white ones, and some people wear white clothing to the synagogue as well. We say special holiday prayers, and we listen to the blowing of the *shofar*.

A shofar is made from the curved horn of a ram. It is

On Rosh Hashanah afternoon, some Jews observe a ceremony called *Tashlich*, which means "throw." They walk to a nearby river or stream and empty their pockets or throw breadcrumbs into the water. The prayer they say is: "You will throw all their sins into the depths of the sea." Tashlich shows that we can empty ourselves of our wrongdoings and make our whole selves clean for the start of a good new year.

TASHLICH *Jewish New Yorkers throw bread crumbs into the Hudson River.*

difficult to blow and has a strong, sharp, unusual sound. The ancient Israelites used a shofar on very important occasions, to call the people to attention. Today, thousands of years later, we are using it in the same way.

The shofar's blast turns our thoughts to many important things. First of all, the shofar's sound is like a trumpet announcing the approach of a king or queen, and when we hear it we think of God, the great King over us all. The sound of the horn is also like a call to action, even to battle. It alerts us and reminds us to pay attention to

14

On Rosh Hashanah we are reminded, by the shofar, of the binding of Isaac. We read the Torah story. God told Abraham to take his son Isaac to a mountaintop and offer him there as a sacrifice. Although Abraham loved Isaac dearly and hated the idea of killing him, he brought Isaac to the place as God commanded. He bound Isaac with ropes and placed him on the altar. But then God called to Abraham, "Do not harm Isaac. Now I know that you are faithful to Me, even when I ask you for your son."

Then Abraham saw a ram, caught in the bushes by its horns. Abraham took the ram and offered it in place of Isaac as a sacrifice to God.

God wanted to test Abraham. But God did not want to make him suffer, or to hurt Isaac. The ram's horn reminds us that God was kind and merciful then just as He is to us now on Rosh Hashanah.

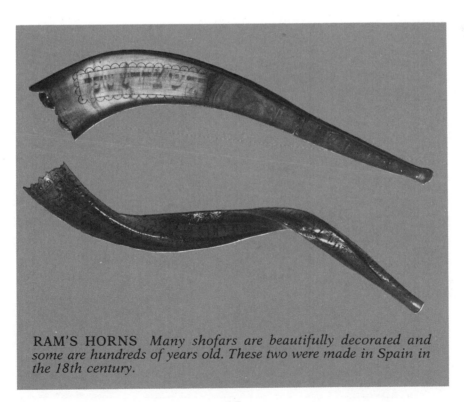

RAM'S HORNS *Many shofars are beautifully decorated and some are hundreds of years old. These two were made in Spain in the 18th century.*

15

THE SHOFAR CALLS

There are three kinds of calls that are blown on the shofar. The first is a long clear blast. It is called *tekiah*. The second is a set of three short notes, called *shevarim*. The third is a fast call made up of nine very short notes in a row; its name is *teruah*. Whenever the shofar is blown, these three kinds of calls are combined in some way.

It is a mitzvah, a commandment of God, for us "to hear the voice of the shofar" on Rosh Hashanah.

our lives. Hearing the shofar also reminds us of another time, long ago, when the shofar sounded at Mount Sinai. God and the Jews made a promise then, always to be loyal to each other. The shofar's sound is also a happy announcement that this is the anniversary of the day the world was created. All of these meanings, and more, we hear in the strange sound of the shofar.

On Rosh Hashanah morning we pray in many ways. We *praise* God, Who is strong and kind. We do something very unusual: we *bow down* to God, to show in the strongest possible way that God is our King. Then we *thank* God for remembering His promise.

And when the Rosh Hashanah service has ended we feel both serious and joyful. We have helped to set the new year off to a good start.

DID YOU KNOW THIS?

Did you know that the Jewish year has not one but many "new years"? Rosh Hashanah is the "birthday of the world," the main new year. But in the spring, at Passover, we celebrate the day when the Jews gained their freedom—their "Independence Day." That's also a new year. It was the Jews' earliest new year, and it is what the Torah calls the new year. Then, in the time of the Kings of Israel, there was also a new year for the government.

In fact, there's even a fourth "new year," the new year of the trees—Tu bi-Shevat.

Mitzvah means "commandment." Through the commandments—not only the Ten Commandments, but many others in the Torah—God has told us how to live. If we live according to God's teaching, we will live good lives. And so mitzvah has also come to mean a "good deed."

On Rosh Hashanah, we think about the times when we did—and when we did not—perform a mitzvah. We promise ourselves that we will perform many more *mitzvot* in the years ahead.

WORDS IN HEBREW

Rosh Hashanah has four Hebrew names. Each one tells us about a different reason for celebrating this especially holy day. These are the names and what they mean:

רֹאשׁ הַשָׁנָה	BEGINNING OF THE YEAR
יוֹם הַזִּכָּרוֹן	DAY OF REMEMBERING
יוֹם הַדִּין	DAY OF JUDGMENT
יוֹם תְּרוּעָה	DAY OF [SOUNDING THE] TERUAH

The last of these names, *Yom Teruah,* reminds us that we are commanded to hear the blowing of the shofar (in Hebrew, שׁוֹפָר). These are the names of the sounds of the shofar:

תְּקִיעָה	TEKIAH
שְׁבָרִים	SHEVARIM
תְּרוּעָה	TERUAH
תְּקִיעָה גְדוֹלָה	TEKIAH GEDOLAH (THE GREAT TEKIAH)

17

Yom Kippur

A Day for
Thinking Hard

Every Jewish year begins with ten days which are the most important days of the whole year. They are called the "Days of Awe." The ten days begin on Rosh Hashanah, the first day of the year. The name of the tenth, final, day is *Yom Kippur*.

"Awe" means "wonder." During the Days of Awe we are filled with wonder, because in our thoughts we are coming closer to God. We wonder at God's greatness: God made us and the whole universe. We wonder at God's kindness: God always hopes that we will do the right things and forgives us when we do the wrong ones.

18

WESTERN WALL *On Yom Kippur, thousands of Jews come to Jerusalem to pray at this wall, which is all that remains of the Second Temple. (See page 163.)*

There is hardly a single empty seat in any synagogue in the world on Yom Kippur.

RIGHT AND WRONG

We know what is right and what is wrong. Our parents and teachers have helped us learn how we should act. But it is God Who gave us the Torah; and the Torah has always told us what is right and wrong. We try to live the way we know we should, but sometimes we make mistakes. Mistakes can lead us into more mistakes—lying, or meanness, or anger. Then, it is as if we are wandering away from goodness, and away from God.

And so when a new year is beginning, we want to make a fresh start. We want to get away from the wrong paths that we've been wandering on, and return to the path we know is right. That is why these ten first days of the year are also called days of *Teshuvah*, which means return. During these days we return, in our thoughts and in our actions, to God.

BEING SORRY

Sometimes it's very hard to think about the things we did that were wrong. But we need to do it, for two reasons. It is the right thing to do. And, it will help us feel better, in the long run.

First we have to admit to ourselves the mistakes we made. We think about why we went wrong, and promise ourselves that in the future we will act in a better way.

Then we try to make up for the unkind things we have done to other people. The best way to do that is by going to them and telling them that we are sorry.

There was a time when Jews went to everyone they knew during the days before Yom Kippur, asking each person to forgive them for any unkind things they had done during the year. This is not so common now. But it's still a good idea to ask forgiveness from others, especially for big wrongs that are weighing on our minds. It's not easy, of course. But the actions that are the most difficult for us to admit are just the ones that we most need to get off our chests. We feel stronger and better about ourselves afterwards.

20

On Rosh Hashanah we reminded ourselves that God is our King and our Judge. Rosh Hashanah is the day when God judges our actions of the past year.

Yom Kippur is the day of asking forgiveness for bad actions. God is kind and full of mercy; ready to forgive us.

And so we say that on Yom Kippur God our King gets up from "the throne of judgment" and sits down on "the throne of mercy."

And on Yom Kippur, the last of the ten days, we show God how sorry we are for the wrongs we have done.

YOM KIPPUR CUSTOMS

Yom Kippur is a day of fasting—not eating. Adults are not supposed to eat or drink anything, from the time that the sun goes down the evening before, until sundown a day later. But children, sick people, and old people are not expected to fast for such a long time.

Yom Kippur is a very solemn and serious day, but it is not sad. Instead it has a kind of holiday excitement about it. On Yom Kippur eve we go to the synagogue. The service begins with a very old, lovely prayer, the *Kol Nidre*. The melody of the Kol Nidre is sad and beautiful, and has touched the hearts of many, many Jews over the centuries.

The Yom Kippur services are the most important of the year—and they are the longest. We begin praying in the evening; we continue the next morning, pray all afternoon, and end just as darkness comes that evening. On Yom Kippur day we read from the Torah twice, in the

21

morning and in the afternoon. And, in the afternoon, we read the old and beautiful story of the prophet Jonah.

THE STORY OF JONAH

God spoke to Jonah. He told Jonah to go to the wicked city of Nineveh and tell the people there that God was angry with them. But Jonah did not want to go. He tried to run away from God by going aboard a ship bound for a distant land.

While Jonah was at sea, a huge storm arose that seemed about to overturn the ship. The sailors knew that God must be angry with someone on board. Then Jonah said, "Throw me out into the sea. It is because of me that this great storm has come." The sailors threw Jonah into the waves, and immediately the sea became calm.

Then God sent a great fish to swallow Jonah. Jonah lived in the belly of the fish for three days. At the end of that time Jonah began to pray, praising God, who had saved his life when he was deep in the ocean.

When God heard Jonah's prayer he made the fish throw Jonah safely up onto dry land.

Then God told Jonah, a second time, to go to Nineveh. This time Jonah obeyed. When the people of Nineveh heard Jonah telling them that God was angry and meant to destroy them, they stopped doing evil things and prayed for forgiveness. God forgave them and decided not to destroy them.

But Jonah was angry that God had saved the people of Nineveh, instead of destroying them. So God taught

Jonah another lesson. A vine grew over Jonah's head, sheltering him from the hot sun. The next day God killed the vine. Again Jonah was angry. Then God said to Jonah, "You felt sorry for the vine, which grew in one night and died in one night; don't you think I should feel sorry for the one hundred and twenty thousand people of Nineveh, who don't know the difference between wrong and right?"

You can see why we read the Book of Jonah on Yom Kippur. It tells us quite a lot about being sorry and forgiving. Jonah didn't want to help save the people of Nineveh, and he didn't want God to save them. But God loves all people, even the wicked ones, and wants to help them become good. God was much more forgiving than Jonah. Jonah had to be taught to be generous to other people. But we can be sure that God will *always* be kind and forgiving.

The Shofar Is Blown One Last Time

The long Yom Kippur service is full of deep emotion. By the time it is finished we feel tired but also overflowing with feeling. The shofar is blown one long, last time. Yom Kippur is over.

The Days of Awe have ended. We feel clean and new; tired, but happy. A good year lies ahead. *Shanah Tovah!* A Good Year!

WHY DO WE FAST?

What is the reason for fasting on Yom Kippur? It is not a punishment; it is not to hurt us in any way. It is also not for showing off, to ourselves or others, that we can do something difficult. The reason we do not eat or drink on Yom Kippur is so that our minds, and our day, will be entirely clear for praying and speaking closely to God. We don't want to take the time to eat, and we don't want to spend our energies on everyday thoughts like food. This day is not like any other day of the year. We have something very important to do, and so we put aside all ordinary things.

Of course, when we feel pangs of hunger we might find it hard not to think of food. But those hunger pangs will help remind us that the day is special and important.

WORDS IN HEBREW

In English, we call this season the "High Holy Days," but in Hebrew, it has another name:

יָמִים נוֹרָאִים   Days of Awe

Yom Kippur, which means Day of Atonement, has a second name which tells us how important the holiday is to us. It is as meaningful as the Sabbath—in fact, it is like a very special Sabbath. Here are the two names in Hebrew:

יוֹם כִּפּוּר   DAY OF ATONEMENT
שַׁבַּת שַׁבָּתוֹן   SABBATH OF SABBATHS

BREAKING THE FAST

After it is dark and the Yom Kippur services are ended, we return to our homes to break the long fast. Together we share a happy meal, knowing that God has forgiven us for our sins.

Some Jews go outside this very night and begin building a *sukkah* for the holiday of SUKKOT. It is a sign of joy, for SUKKOT is one of the happiest days of the Jewish year.

25

Sukkot

Sukkot means "booths" or "huts." The holiday has this name because of the booths we build as part of our celebration.

Sukkot is a harvest holiday. It marks the time when the summer's crops are ripened and harvested. People everywhere have always celebrated harvest time. Thanksgiving is the American harvest holiday.

For us today, it is hard to see the importance of the harvest. We buy fresh fruit and vegetables all year long, because during the winter these foods are shipped to us

26

from warmer places. We seldom see how our food grows. We don't pay much attention to the time when it ripens and is gathered.

IN ANCIENT DAYS

But, in the days of the Bible, most Jews were farmers. They spent quite a lot of time and energy working to produce food. They worried about whether there would be enough rain, or whether disease would injure their plants. When the crops were finally ripe, the farmers worked without resting; they had to harvest the crop before it spoiled.

When the harvest was in at last, the farmers were exhausted but also filled with joy. They were grateful to God and proud of their own work. Now they could relax and know there would be food, because they had done their job well. This was the happiest time of the year for them. They called it "the Happy Season."

The Jews of Bible times usually lived in small villages. Every day they trudged out to work in their fields, which spread out far beyond the village. During the day they sometimes rested in little booths to get out of the sun. But during the harvest season there was such an enormous amount of work to be done, and so little time in which to do it, the farmers didn't want to waste time walking out to their fields each morning and back to their homes at night. So they used their little huts out in the fields as "homes away from home." They worked from sunup until dark and lived in their booths until the entire crop was gathered. To remember their good work we

27

Building a sukkah in Israel.

build our own booths, or *sukkot*, when we celebrate this holiday.

SUKKOT IN THE DESERT

Harvesting is something that all farmers do, everywhere. But there is another reason, an especially Jewish reason, for building booths at Sukkot. After Moses led the Jews out of Egypt they wandered for forty years in the desert before they reached the land of Israel; and during this time, God told them to build booths for themselves. In these simple huts, which they set up as they traveled from place to place, the Israelites found protection from the burning sun of the day and cold desert nights.

And so we build booths for *two* reasons. But the two reasons fit together to become one, larger reason: God provides for us. With God's protection, we survived forty years in the desert and reached our homeland; by God's generosity, all kinds of food for us grows out of the earth. We need to work hard to make our lives good, just as the Jews of the Bible did—but we know that God will always be there to help us.

SUKKOT CUSTOMS

In the Torah, God tells us how to celebrate Sukkot. "You shall rejoice," the Torah says, and "you shall live in booths for seven days."

It used to be that people ate all their meals in the sukkah during the entire holiday of Sukkot. Some people even slept in the sukkah. Today, because of the way most of us live, it is very difficult to live for seven days in a sukkah—although some Jews still do.

You can go to the sukkah built by your synagogue. Perhaps a meal will be served in the sukkah; otherwise, there will be a blessing and a little snack—a *Kiddush*.

When we eat in a sukkah we can imagine, a little, what these times were like for our ancestors. We think of them traveling for years through the desert, depending only on God for protection. We feel grateful that God brought them to a land where they could settle and grow food out of the earth. We think of the Israelites' determination and the hard work they did, farming and harvesting. Finally we feel the happiness, thankfulness, and holiday excitement that they felt when their work was done. That was when they celebrated, as we do now—thousands of years later—"the Happy Season."

Celebrating The Happy Season

It's now lunchtime! This sukkah is in California.

BUILDING A SUKKAH

"Living" in a sukkah on Sukkot is a mitzvah—a commandment, and a good deed. Maybe you will be able to help build a sukkah for your family in your yard, or a large one at your synagogue. A sukkah is not a heavy, solid building. The whole idea of a sukkah is that it is only meant to stand for a little while. The walls can be built in almost any way; a sukkah can even be built on top of a building that is already standing, or along the side of one. But the sukkah's roof is special. It is always made of leafy branches, with spaces between them so that at night you can see the stars.

Decorating the sukkah is probably the most fun of all. Hang fruits, vegetables, gourds, and flowers all around the sukkah. Then the sukkah will look beautiful and smell wonderful. And of course, these decorations show that Sukkot is a harvest holiday. You can also make all sorts of decorations out of paper or clay to hang in the sukkah.

You can build a miniature sukkah to put in the center of your family's table. Make it out of a cardboard or wooden box, with the top taken off. Cut windows and a door. Use little leafy branches for the roof, and inside hang cranberries, grapes, raisins, and other small fruits (you can string them with a needle and thread).

Or perhaps you will build a sukkah in your mind. There are many ways to have a sukkah—a real one to eat in, a small one on your table, or one that you carry around in your head. What's important is the idea of a sukkah—something that protects us, but still is open to the sky.

WORDS IN HEBREW

The word for a joyous holiday in Hebrew is חַג, which means "festival." In ancient times, when most Jews were farmers, Sukkot was the most important festival of the year. They called it *The* Festival, for short. But they had other names for it, too. Here they are:

הֶחָג	THE FESTIVAL
זְמַן שִׂמְחָתֵנוּ	SEASON OF OUR HAPPINESS
חַג הָאָסִיף	FESTIVAL OF HARVEST
סֻכּוֹת	(THE HOLIDAY OF) BOOTHS

30

Sukkot

The Beautiful World

The Bible tells us that on Sukkot we should "take the fruit of fine trees, and the branches of palm trees, and the boughs of leafy trees and willows of the brook"; with these we will "rejoice before the Lord for seven days." These four different kinds of growing things are symbols. A symbol is something that reminds us of something else; and these four symbols remind us of all the beautiful growing things in the world. That is why we use them to celebrate the harvest.

ARBA'AH MINIM—THE FOUR KINDS

The four symbols are four special plants. The fruit of a fine—or "goodly"—tree is a citron, or *etrog*, which looks like a large lemon. It has a special aroma all its own. The other three symbols are all branches of trees. The branch of a palm tree, or *lulav*, is tall and slender, almost like a sword. The "leafy tree" is a myrtle (*hadasim*) tree, whose leaves are small, oval, and sweet-smelling. The willow (*aravot*), with its long thin leaves, has a feathery look.

These three kinds of branches are carefully bound together. The tall palm branch is in the center. On one side of it are three myrtle branches, and on the other side two willow branches. The bottoms of all the branches fit into a little holder made of woven palm leaves. The whole bundle is called a *lulav*, because the lulav is its tallest part.

When Sukkot is coming, many people buy an etrog

LULAV *Greens for the lulavim are collected in the fields. Buying a lulav at a Jerusalem market.*

and lulav to use in the Sukkot services. At every morning service, while the members of the congregation say a special blessing, they point the etrog and lulav in all four directions, then up and down. Each time the etrog and lulav are pointed, they are slowly waved three times. By observing this very old ceremony we are saying, in a simple, beautiful way, that God is everywhere.

A spice box made in the shape of an etrog.

During another part of the service, in some synagogues, everyone parades around the synagogue carrying etrogim and lulavim. As we march, we recite blessings in praise of God, and also prayers to God to help us. On the seventh day of Sukkot, instead of parading once, everyone marches seven times around, reciting prayers and calling out "Hoshana." (*Hoshana* means "God, help us.") That is why the seventh day of Sukkot is called *Hoshana Rabbah*, the Great Hoshana.

THE ENDING OF SUKKOT

The final day of Sukkot has its own name, *Shemini Atzeret*. This day is different from the rest. We do not wave the etrog and lulav. Instead of being festive we are a little solemn. We are slowly letting go of the joyous Sukkot holiday.

A special ceremony takes place on this day, a prayer for rain. To the Israelite farmers, living in a dry land, this was enormously important. If there wasn't enough rain during the fall rainy season, their crops would not grow well the following spring.

Up until now, the Sukkot celebration has been one of

ETROG *An etrog is best if it has no spots. These Israelis carefully look over their etrogim before buying.*

thanks for the harvest already completed. But the prayer for rain is a prayer for the *future*, asking God to take care of the Jews as in the past. Now, in this country, we seldom need to pray for rain; but we never stop needing to pray for God's care, and so we repeat the same words our ancestors repeated:

> For You are the Lord our God,
> Who makes the wind blow and the rain fall . . .
> מַשִּׁיב הָרוּחַ וּמוֹרִיד הַגָּשֶׁם.
> Sukkot is over, until next year.

34

Together the lulav and etrog are called the *four species*, which means four kinds. We have seen that they are symbols of the harvest. But over the centuries the four species have reminded people of many other ideas as well. According to one theory, the lulav and etrog are like different parts of the *body*. The etrog is the heart; the straight palm is the backbone; the myrtle, with its oval leaves, is the eyes; and the willow is the mouth. Put them all together and they make a whole person who is able to harvest crops and then give thanks to God.

There is another idea that the four species are like people. The etrog, myrtle, willow, and palm are all different—they have different shapes, different smells, different ways of growing. In the same way, people are different, no two alike, each with special strengths and weaknesses. But just as we bring the four species together because they are all part of the growing world, in the same way all of us—different as we are—belong together as part of the Jewish people. Together we become something greater than ourselves, something important and strong.

Try to make up your own idea of what the four species stand for and why we bring them together.

HAKHEL *These Jews are lighting candles beside King David's Tomb–on Mount Zion in Jerusalem–as part of the ceremony of "hakhel." Hakhel is an assembly of the people which takes place every seven years, on the second day of Sukkot.*

DOES WORK MAKE YOU HAPPY?

On the Shabbat that falls during Sukkot, we read a book of the Bible called *Kohelet*, Ecclesiastes. The author of this book believed that many things we try to get turn out to be disappointing once we get them. But one thing in life he knew was important:

"There is nothing better than for a person to rejoice in work. . . . For every person to eat and drink, and enjoy pleasure in return for labor, is the gift of God."

That hard work of a whole year, ending in the harvest, was what Jews rejoiced in, long ago, on Sukkot.

Do you agree that the pleasure you get from having done a big job well is one of the best feelings you can have? Could that be what is meant by "the gift of God"?

WORDS IN HEBREW

On Sukkot, we use four growing things that together are called the "four kinds," or, in Hebrew אַרְבָּעָה מִינִים. Here are their names:

אֶתְרוֹג	CITRON
לוּלָב	PALM BRANCH
הֲדַסִּים	MYRTLE BRANCHES
עֲרָבוֹת	WILLOW BRANCHES

Simḥat Torah

Beginning the Torah Again

Simḥat Torah comes the day after Sukkot, but it is a quite separate holiday. Its name means "rejoicing for the Torah," and it may be the happiest holiday in the whole year.

The Torah is a handwritten scroll that we read little by little, all through the year. Each week, a section, or "portion," of the Torah is read aloud in the synagogue. Parts of the weekly portion are read on Monday, Thursday, and Shabbat. It takes exactly a year for us to read the entire Torah. And when we have finished, we go right back to the beginning and start to read it all over again!

Simḥat Torah is a holiday because it is the day on which we finish reading the Torah. On the same day, we

37

turn to the Torah's beginning and read its first chapter. That makes it a perfect day for celebrating. The Torah is the most precious thing we have, and on Simhat Torah we show how glad we are to have it.

SIMHAT TORAH EVE

The evening of Simhat Torah is a little like a party. Everyone comes to the synagogue. There the rabbi takes all the Torah scrolls out of the Ark, giving each one to a different person. Then there is a great parade around the synagogue. Those who carry the Torah scrolls lead the way and the children follow, carrying flags or miniature scrolls. Everyone is singing.

Each procession around the synagogue is called a *hakkafah*. Altogether there are seven *hakkafot* on Simhat Torah eve. Each time, different members of the congregation have a turn to carry the scrolls. People reach out to touch a Torah scroll, or kiss it, as it is carried by. And after all the singing and celebration, there are many good things to eat.

In earlier times, and in some synagogues even today, people were so excited on Simhat Torah that they not only paraded but danced with the scrolls. They danced around the synagogue and out into the street. In Israel today, on Simhat Torah eve, the streets are filled with people dancing. They sing and shout and dance far into the night.

THE DAY OF SIMHAT TORAH

The next morning, on Simhat Torah day, there are again processions in the synagogue. Then it is time to read from

Hakkafah
A Torah scroll parade around the
synagogue on Simhat Torah eve.

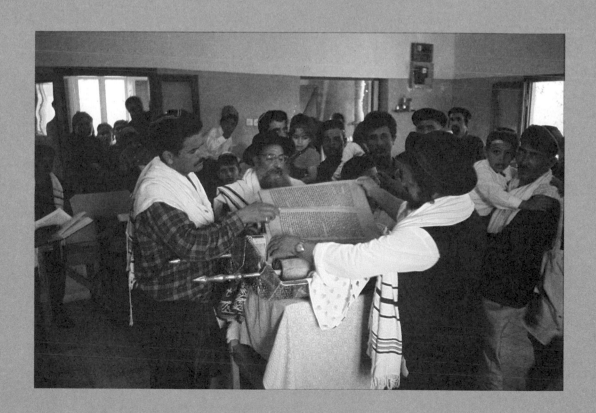

SIMHAT TORAH MORNING *The children say a blessing over the Torah in the shelter of the tallit held above them.*

the Torah—first the very last chapters, and then, from a different scroll, the very first chapter. People are called up to say the *berachot*, blessings, over the Torah for each part of the reading.

One of the blessings over the Torah is said by all the children younger than Bar or Bat Mitzvah age. They stand together at the front of the synagogue, and often a large *tallit*, or prayer shawl, is held over their heads. Then an adult leads them in saying the blessings.

It is a special honor to be called up to the Torah for the last verses of the Torah. A man who is asked to do this is called the *Ḥatan Torah*, the "bridegroom of the Torah."

The final chapters of the Torah, which we read on Simḥat Torah, are about Moses. After Moses had brought the Israelites to the very edge of the Promised Land, God told him to climb a mountain. From the top, Moses could see stretched before him the land that would become Israel. Moses knew he would not live to enter that land. So Moses blessed all the Israelites, and then he died. For many days the people mourned for him. Then they moved on toward the land that had been promised to them by God.

When we read this we feel saddened by the death of our greatest leader, but we also feel glad. This final chapter of the Torah is about endings and beginnings—the end of the Jews' first long wandering, the end of Moses' life, and also the beginning of the Jewish people's new life in their own land.

After we finish the Torah, we turn back to its beginning to read the first chapter. This chapter takes us far back, to the very beginning of *everything*. We read how, out of nothingness, God created the heaven and the earth. First God made day and night. Then He made the sky and earth and ocean, and the sun and moon and stars, and plants and animals, and finally human beings. Then God rested, because the work of Creation was done.

Reading about Creation after reading the Torah's last chapters makes us think about everything that comes between. The same God Who created everything that exists also taught Abraham to worship One God. In Abraham the Jews had their beginning. They grew and struggled. In the time of Joseph they came to live in Egypt. There they were enslaved. But God brought them out of Egypt under Moses' leadership. Then God gave the Jews a great gift, the Ten Commandments. After that the Jews wandered for many years, but finally they reached their own land. There they would become a nation.

The Torah tells us who we are and where we come from. Those things are too important to forget. And so on Simḥat Torah we turn back to the beginning, to start reading it all again.

"REJOICING IN THE TORAH" *These paintings convey the joy and excitement of traditional dancing with the Torah on Simḥat Torah eve.*

A man who says the blessing over the beginning chapter that is read next is also honored: he is *Ḥatan Bereshit*, the "bridegroom of the beginning." By using the word *Ḥatan*, "bridegroom," we show how great our love is for the Torah. We love it as deeply as people about to be married love each other. We also show how happy and excited we are on this day, as happy as we would be at a wedding.

All this wonderful excitement over the Torah reminds us again that the Torah is very special. The Torah is our Book of Books. It tells us about God, our special agreement with God, and our history; and it teaches us how to live. That's why we read it over and over, each year, and why we celebrate it with such joy on Simḥat Torah.

WORDS IN HEBREW

Here are three Hebrew words which will help you to remember this holiday. One is the holiday's name, one is the special gift we celebrate on this day, and one is how we do our celebrating.

תּוֹרָה	TORAH, THE FIVE BOOKS OF MOSES
שִׂמְחַת תּוֹרָה	REJOICING FOR THE TORAH
הַקָּפָה	PROCESSION, A MARCH AROUND THE SYNAGOGUE

Shabbat

Rest and
Freedom

Shabbat, the Sabbath, is different from all the other holidays. We celebrate those holidays only once each year. But Shabbat comes every week. We know it very well. Shabbat is familiar and close to us, like a member of the family or a good friend.

We refer to the Sabbath not as "it" but as "she." That's because we think of the Shabbat as a queen. The Sabbath day is not only a good friend whom we love, but also a special, beautiful, shining day that makes everything around it special, too—the "queen" of days. Every seventh day we are blessed because then the Shabbat queen, kind and loving, visits us.

SHABBAT—A DAY OF REST

We read about Shabbat in the very beginning of the Bible. God began to make the world out of nothingness. Each day He made something new: light and darkness; heaven, earth, and ocean; trees and plants; the sun, moon, and stars; fish, birds, and animals; and finally, men and women. By the end of six days God had finished making the entire world and everything in it.

Then God looked at what He had made and saw that it was very good. And on the seventh day God did not work; He rested. God blessed the seventh day and declared it holy, because on that day He stopped and rested from His work.

Reading about that first Sabbath helps us understand what the Sabbath really is. It is a time for *stopping* our everyday activity. On Shabbat we do no work. When we stop our usual work and play we have a chance, not only to rest, but also to think. We can look back over what we have done, as God did, and see whether it has been good. It's hard to tell, in the midst of busy days, whether all the

Young and old celebrate Shabbat.

things we spend our time on really make sense. But when we draw back from our daily round, into a little island of quiet, we are able to understand much more about our lives. Suddenly we can tell which things we do are important and which hardly matter.

And when we observe the Sabbath, when we stop all our usual work and busyness, something wonderful happens. We feel ourselves gradually being filled with peace and calm. It is as if our souls have more room to breathe. We can feel all our emotions more clearly—love for our parents, family, and friends, and happiness at just being alive.

SHABBAT—A DAY OF FREEDOM

Shabbat is found in the Bible not only in the story of Creation, but in another very important place as well: it is one of the Ten Commandments. "Observe the Sabbath day and keep it holy," says the fourth commandment. "Remember that you were a slave in the land of Egypt, and the Lord your God freed you." For a slave there is no

SHABBAT HAS BEEN OUR FRIEND

In the many times when life has been hard for Jews, Shabbat was the small shining light that kept them going. When Friday night came they put aside their worries and welcomed the Sabbath queen. They turned their thoughts to their families and friends and drew strength from the love they shared; they studied Torah and Talmud and drew strength from thinking about God's wisdom and love. Although the world outside was unfriendly, in their homes and synagogues they were safe in an island of peace and love. When Shabbat came to an end they felt rested and strengthened for the difficult week that lay before them.

Havdalah
(The end of Shabbat)

This woodcut illustration comes from a book of Jewish ceremonies that is nearly three hundred years old.

day of rest, only endless work. To be able to keep Shabbat is the privilege of a free person. On this day we are free to put aside our usual weekday worries.

Today we are not slaves to other masters, as the Israelites were slaves to the Egyptians. But sometimes we make ourselves slaves to our own work or even to our play—we get so busy with things to do, things to finish, places to go, that it seems we don't have a moment to breathe. When that happens, we are letting the things we do be master over us—and it should be the other way around.

And so we need the Sabbath. It helps us to have this special island of time set aside from the rest of the week. In keeping Shabbat we grow strong and rested, and we become free. Shabbat is for us.

There is an old legend that God said, "I have a precious jewel which I am going to give to the Jewish people. The name of the jewel is Shabbat."

WORDS IN HEBREW

Shabbat is the only holiday commanded in the Ten Commandments. In Hebrew the Ten Commandments are known by two different names. They are called the ten "words" or "things," and they are called the "tablets of the Covenant." A convenant is an agreement; the Covenant with a capital *C* is the agreement between God and the Jewish people that was made at Mount Sinai. Shabbat is an important part of that agreement.

שַׁבָּת   (DAY OF) REST, SABBATH

עֲשֶׂרֶת הַדִּבְּרוֹת   THE TEN STATEMENTS

לוּחוֹת הַבְּרִית   THE TABLETS OF THE COVENANT

Shabbat

Welcoming
the Sabbath Shabbat begins at sundown on Friday evening. In a home where Shabbat is observed, the mother lights the Sabbath candles just before Shabbat begins. There are usually two candles, and sometimes more, because a holiday should be celebrated with more than a single candle. After lighting the Sabbath candles, the mother sometimes moves her hands around the candles and toward her face several times. This is an old custom with many meanings. Some say it is a gesture of welcome to the Sabbath queen. The mother holds her hands before her eyes, shielding them from the light, and recites the blessing over the Sabbath candles.

49

THE SHABBAT CANDLES

The blessing for kindling the Sabbath candles is:

בָּרוּךְ אַתָּה, יְיָ אֱלֹהֵינוּ, מֶלֶךְ הָעוֹלָם, אֲשֶׁר קִדְּשָׁנוּ בְּמִצְוֹתָיו
וְצִוָּנוּ לְהַדְלִיק נֵר שֶׁל שַׁבָּת.

*Baruch atah adonai elohenu melech ha-olam asher kidshanu
b'mitzvotav v'tzivanu l'hadlik ner shel shabbat.*

Blessed are You, Lord our God, King of the universe, Who has
made us holy by giving us His commandments, and has
commanded us to kindle the Sabbath lights.

Why does a woman shield her eyes from the candle light while reciting this blessing?

Usually we say a blessing just *before* we do a certain thing—for instance, we say a
blessing over bread and then eat the bread. But we can't do that with the Shabbat
candles, because lighting a candle is a kind of work that shouldn't be done on Shabbat.
Since Shabbat begins when we say the blessing, lighting the candles *after* that would be
lighting them on Shabbat. That's why a woman lights the candles *before* she says the
blessing. But then she covers her eyes until she has said the blessing. So, in a way, the
candlelight doesn't really "appear" until after the blessing.

THE FRIDAY EVENING SERVICE

In the synagogue, we also welcome Shabbat. The traditional Friday evening service begins at sundown. It in-
cludes the poems and songs welcoming Shabbat. One of
these, *Lechah Dodee*, means "Come, my beloved"; in this
song, the Sabbath is compared with a beautiful bride. As
the members of the congregation sing the last verse, they
stand and turn to face the entrance of the synagogue,
through which the Sabbath bride will "enter." When the
song is finished, Shabbat has been welcomed in.

50

After the service people wish each other "Shabbat Shalom" (in Hebrew, "A peaceful Sabbath") or "Gut Shabbes" (in Yiddish, "Good Sabbath").

Shabbat evening at home is festive. The table is set with the best tablecloth and dishes. Everyone wears good clothes. When the family is gathered, the father and mother bless their children.

At the start of the Shabbat meal, the father says the Kiddush—the blessing over wine. Often there is a specially decorated silver Kiddush cup. The Kiddush is long, because it starts with an explanation of Shabbat: that God finished the creation and then rested on the seventh day, and declared the Sabbath *Kadosh*, holy. When the Kiddush is finished, everyone has a sip of wine.

Next comes the blessing over bread. On the Shabbat table are two loaves of ḥallah, the beautiful twisted holiday bread. The loaves are covered with a cloth. The father uncovers them, cuts one, and gives each person a piece.

THE KIDDUSH

The most familiar part of the Kiddush is the blessing over the wine itself:

בָּרוּךְ אַתָּה, יְיָ אֱלֹהֵינוּ, מֶלֶךְ הָעוֹלָם, בּוֹרֵא פְּרִי הַגָּפֶן.

Baruch atah adonai elohenu melech ha-olam boray p'ri hagafen.

Blessed are You, Lord our God, King of the universe, Who creates the fruit of the vine.

ḤALLAH

The blessing over ḥallah is:

בָּרוּךְ אַתָּה, יְיָ אֱלֹהֵינוּ, מֶלֶךְ הָעוֹלָם, הַמּוֹצִיא לֶחֶם מִן הָאָרֶץ.

Baruch atah adonai elohenu melech ha-olam ha-motzi lehem min ha-aretz.

Blessed are You, Lord our God, King of the universe, Who brings forth bread from the earth.

We use two loaves of ḥallah to show that this is a special day; one loaf of bread goes with an everyday meal, but two loaves belong with a feast. Two loaves also help us remember that our ancestors, once they were freed from slavery, rested on Shabbat. When the Israelites were wandering in the wilderness, God sent down *manna* each day for them to eat. But before every Shabbat God sent down a double portion of manna. Then the Israelites could gather two days' worth of manna before Shabbat, and did not need to work gathering food on the Shabbat.

Before eating the ḥallah, everyone recites the blessing to God Who "brings forth bread from the earth."

Now it is time for the meal, a Shabbat meal of the family's favorite special foods. Afterward come the blessings called *Birkat Hamazon*, the grace after meals, and the singing of Shabbat songs.

SABBATH DAY

Saturday, Shabbat day, is a day unlike the rest of the week. People who keep Shabbat do not work or make work plans or talk about business on this day. Cooking, shopping, traveling busily around are not done on the Sabbath. This day is reserved for being with God, with

PREPARING FOR THE SABBATH *Nothing tastes as good as fresh baked ḥallah and nothing is more fun than preparing it together.*

family and friends, and even for being alone; for relaxing, praying, and thinking.

On Sabbath morning many people go to services in the synagogue. This is the most important service of the week. A portion of the Torah is read. On Shabbat, people announce important events to the congregation—for instance, a young couple might announce that they will be married, or a newborn baby might be named. Sometimes on Shabbat a Bar or Bat Mitzvah is celebrated.

READING FROM THE TORAH *Anyone who can read Hebrew can read from the Torah. The silver pointer is called a "yad."*

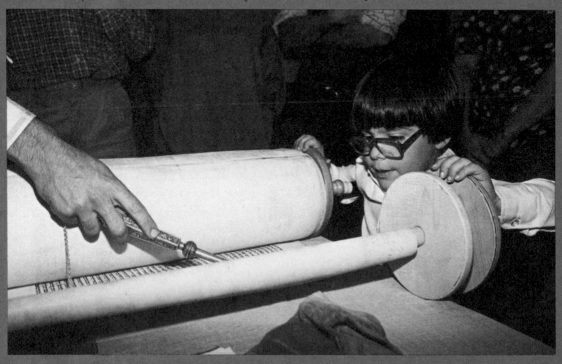

An embroidered hallah cover.

MAKING ḤALLAH

If you make your own ḥallah, Shabbat will seem even more special. Here is a recipe to try.

ḤALLAH

4 tablespoons margarine	2 packages yeast
½ cup sugar	1 cup warm water
1 tablespoon salt	2 eggs
1 cup boiling water	5 cups flour

1. Put the margarine, sugar, salt, and boiling water in a large bowl and stir until completely mixed. Put the yeast and warm water in a small bowl and stir until the yeast dissolves. Then pour the yeast mixture into the large bowl and stir well. Beat the eggs in a separate bowl, then pour them into the large bowl and stir everything again. Next, add the flour, little by little, and mix well. That's your dough.

2. Turn the dough out onto a floured table or board. Oil your hands (to keep the dough from sticking), and knead the dough for about ten minutes. Knead by pushing on it with the heel of your hands, turning the dough over, pushing again, over and over. If the dough is too sticky, add a little more flour.

3. Oil a large bowl and put the dough in it. Cover the bowl with a towel and put it in a warm corner of the kitchen until the dough rises and is twice as big as it was before. Put it into the refrigerator overnight.

4. The next day, take out the dough. Put it on the table, punch it down, and knead it a little. Divide it into two or three parts for loaves.

5. For each loaf, divide the dough into three pieces. Roll each piece into a long, even snake. Now pinch the three strands together at one end and braid them. Pinch the other end then the braid is complete.

6. Let the loaves rise until they are twice as big as before. If you want the ḥallah to be shiny, brush the loaves with a little beaten egg. Then bake them at 400° until they're brown.

In homes where the Sabbath is strictly observed there is no cooking on this day. Yet Shabbat lunch can be a real feast. How? It can be *cholent*, a dish that has been baking slowly in the warm oven since Friday afternoon.

In the afternoon there is time to relax, to take walks, to visit with friends, or even to take a nap. The rabbis used to say that a Jew has something even a king does not have. A king can never lay down his worries completely, and enjoy a real rest. But we can—we have Shabbat.

Shabbat

Shabbat Comes to an End

When three stars can be seen in the sky, or after the sun has set, it is time to say goodbye to Shabbat. We do this with a special ceremony called *Havdalah*, which means "separation."

A beautiful large candle made of several strands of wax braided or twisted together is used for the Havdalah ceremony. A child may hold the candle, which is lit before the ceremony begins. On the table is a cup of wine filled to overflowing, with a plate beneath it. The father lifts the cup and says the blessing over wine.

HAVDALAH *The havdalah candle has just been lit and the wine is ready in the cup.*

BESAMIM BOXES *These spice boxes are made to look like castles. The left-hand one is of silver, the right-hand one of carved wood.*

The blessing over spices is:

בָּרוּךְ אַתָּה, יְיָ אֱלֹהֵינוּ, מֶלֶךְ הָעוֹלָם, בּוֹרֵא מִינֵי בְשָׂמִים.

Baruch atah adonai elohenu melech ha-olam boray minay b'samim.

Blessed are You, Lord our God, King of the Universe, Who creates all kinds of spices.

The blessing over the Havdalah candle is:

בָּרוּךְ אַתָּה, יְיָ אֱלֹהֵינוּ, מֶלֶךְ הָעוֹלָם, בּוֹרֵא מְאוֹרֵי הָאֵשׁ.

Baruch atah adonai elohenu melech ha-olam boray m'oray haesh.

Blessed are You, Lord our God, King of the Universe, Who creates the light of the fire.

The first part of the Havdalah blessing is:

בָּרוּךְ אַתָּה, יְיָ אֱלֹהֵינוּ, מֶלֶךְ הָעוֹלָם, הַמַּבְדִּיל בֵּין קֹדֶשׁ לְחֹל, בֵּין אוֹר לְחֹשֶׁךְ.

Baruch atah adonai elohenu melech ha-olam hamavdil bayn kodesh l'ḥol, bayn or l'ḥoshech.

Blessed are You, Lord our God, King of the Universe, Who divides the holy from the ordinary, the light from the darkness.

SPICE AND LIGHT

Also on the table is a spice box (*besamim* box). This is a special container, often made of silver. Sometimes it is in the shape of a tiny castle tower, with windows and roof ornaments. The spice box has holes to let out the sweet fragrance of the spices inside. The father lifts the spice box and says the blessing over it. Then he passes the box around, so that everyone can have a whiff of its warm, spicy aroma. It is as if we are taking a last breath of Sabbath sweetness, to keep with us throughout the week.

Now the father takes up the Havdalah candle and says a blessing over it: "Blessed be God Who creates the light of fire." When God created the world, His first deed was to say, "Let there be light." Since the first thing done on the very first day was God's creation of light, we say a blessing over light at this very beginning of the first day of the week.

Then we hold our hands before the candle light, opening and closing them so that we can feel the warmth of the candle's flame and see the movement of light and shadow. The difference between the bright light and the dark shadow is like the difference between holy Shabbat and the rest of the week. It is the separation between these two that we celebrate with the Havdalah ceremony.

A TIME OF SEPARATION

Now the father lifts up the cup again to say the words of "separation" (Havdalah). He blesses God Who divides

> light from darkness,
> Israel from the other nations,
> Shabbat from the six days of work.
> Blessed are You, God, Who separates the holy from the ordinary.

Everyone takes a sip of wine from the cup. Then the father puts out the Havdalah candle by dipping its flame in the wine that has overflowed onto the plate. Shabbat is over.

We sing together to wish each other a good week— *Shavua Tov* in Hebrew, *A Gut Voch* in Yiddish. Another traditional song to sing at this time is "Elijah the Prophet," *Eliyahu Hanavi*.

At the close of Shabbat we feel peaceful and strong. We are sad at having to let go of the beautiful, holy Sabbath, the sweet spicy Sabbath, the queenly Sabbath we love. But we also feel filled with quiet happiness. We have rested and studied Torah and thought about God and

Everyone joins in the Havdalah ceremony.

about ourselves, and this has strengthened us. We are ready for what comes next; we will carry a little bit of Shabbat with us into the week ahead.

WORDS IN HEBREW

When we say goodbye to Shabbat, we make a separation between the Sabbath and the six ordinary days of the week. And we sing two songs: one tells of our hope that God will send the prophet Elijah; the other expresses our hope for a good week ahead. Here are the Hebrew words for these things:

הַבְדָּלָה   SEPARATION, (THE CEREMONY OF) HAVDALAH

אֵלִיָהוּ הַנָבִיא   THE PROPHET ELIJAH

שָׁבוּעַ טוֹב!   A GOOD WEEK!

Shabbat

Beloved
Shabbat

A story is told about a wise rabbi, Joshua ben Hananiah, who lived almost two thousand years ago. The Emperor Hadrian, who ruled the mighty Roman Empire, sometimes met with Rabbi Joshua to talk and argue. One Sabbath evening the emperor stayed for dinner at Joshua's house. He was amazed to find that the food was marvelous, the most delicious he had ever tasted. "What makes this food taste so extraordinary?" Hadrian asked Joshua.

"We have a special spice, called Sabbath, which is put in with the meat as it cooks," Joshua replied.

"Give me some of that spice," said the emperor.

"That I cannot do," Joshua answered. "The spice adds flavor only where people keep the Sabbath: in a home that has no Sabbath, the spice will not work at all."

The story shows something important. It is the loving feeling we have toward Shabbat that makes everything about this day, including the food, seem very special. There is no quick and easy way to get that specialness; you cannot buy it, borrow it, or bring it home in a box. Only when we give ourselves to Shabbat does Shabbat give us something precious in return.

THE FEELING OF SHABBAT

For Jews over the centuries, the precious gift of the Sabbath has been very important. When life was hard and the world was frightening or unfriendly, Shabbat was the day on which Jews could feel whole again. They turned their minds away from the outside world and drew closer to their families and to God. This gave them strength to go on, not to be discouraged, to work for better times. In fact, it has been said, "More than the Jews kept the Sabbath, the Sabbath has kept the Jews."

In earlier days, even the poorest families would serve a special dinner on Shabbat; they scrimped and saved and sometimes skipped meals during the week to be able to set a Sabbath table. Then, for one day of the week, they felt free and rich, able to entertain the Sabbath queen. And when the Sabbath queen came to visit, each family felt that its simple home had turned into a palace.

Because Shabbat has always been so beloved, many

stories and legends have grown up about it. Here is one:

The Sabbath is a day that stands alone. All the other days go in pairs—the first and second day go together, the third and fourth day go together, and so do the fifth and sixth day. But Shabbat, the seventh day, has no partner. Shabbat was lonely and said to God, "Please give me a partner. All the other days have partners; I alone do not." God replied, "The people Israel will be your partner."

STUDYING ON SHABBAT

Any ordinary kind of studying—doing your school homework, for instance—is work, which would not be done on Shabbat. But studying about the Torah is different. It is a way of coming closer to God, and that makes it a very good Shabbat activity. Some families have this custom: each Shabbat the parents ask their children to tell what they have been learning in Hebrew school during the week.

Some adults like to spend Shabbat afternoon studying the Torah or reading the writings of the rabbis. Often they read from a book called *Sayings of the Fathers* (*Pirke Avot*), in which there are gathered the sayings of many wise rabbis. The sayings are about how to live. Anyone who ever wonders, "How should I act? What should I do to become the kind of person I want to be?" will find many ideas to think about in this book—ideas written centuries ago that still make us think today.

For instance, Rabbi Eleazar used to say,

A person who knows a great deal but does not do very much, what is that person like? Like a tree with many branches but only a few roots: the wind will come and pluck it up and turn it over onto its face. But the person who does many good things, even without knowing a great deal, what is that person like? Like a tree with few branches but many roots: all the winds in the world cannot move it from its place.

The famous Rabbi Hillel used to say,

If I am not for myself, who will be for me? But if I am only for myself, what kind of person am I? And if I do not do things now, when will I?

Words like these encourage us to try to be our best possible selves.

The saying of a rabbi with a rather unusual name, Rabbi Ben Bag Bag, reminds us of where our knowledge comes from:

Turn the Torah over and turn it over again, for everything is in it; and think about it, and grow old with it, and do not leave it, for you can have no better guide than this.

Learning the wise, generous lessons that have helped many people before us is another good way to help ourselves on Shabbat.

Pesaḥ

Holiday
of Freedom

Passover is the holiday of freedom. Every part of the Passover celebration helps to tell this fact: the Jews were slaves, and God brought us out of slavery into freedom.

How this happened is told in the second book of the Torah, Exodus, which means "going out." Here is the story.

The Israelites came to Egypt in Joseph's time. They lived there peacefully and had many children. But years later a new king, or pharaoh, enslaved them and forced them to do backbreaking work with mortar and heavy bricks.

Pharaoh was worried, because even in slavery the Jews grew more and more numerous. So he ordered every

67

boy child born to the Israelites to be thrown into the river and drowned. But one Jewish woman placed her baby boy in a little basket and set the basket afloat at the river's edge. There the baby was found by Pharaoh's daughter who took him into her care and named him *Moshe*, Moses.

MOSES GROWS UP

Moses grew up like a prince, in Pharaoh's palace. In time, he learned that he was Jewish. He began to watch his fellow Jews, slaving for the Egyptians. One day he saw an Egyptian foreman whipping an Israelite. Moses became so angry that he struck the Egyptian, killing him. Then, afraid of revenge from Pharaoh, Moses fled from Egypt. He came to the land of Midian, where he married and became a shepherd.

One day in the desert, Moses saw a bush that was on fire but was not burned by the flames. Then, from the bush, God spoke. "Moses," said the Lord, "I have seen the suffering of My people in Egypt. I am going to rescue them from the Egyptians and bring them to a good land. I am

WHY "PASSOVER"?

Before sending the last plague down on the Egyptians, God warned Moses, saying, "Tell the people in every Jewish family to kill a young lamb. Have them put some of the blood on the doorposts of their houses; then let them roast the lamb and eat it. At night I will come through Egypt. I will strike dead the firstborn of every Egyptian family and of every animal. But when I see the blood on your doorposts I will pass over your houses, and you will be saved."

That is why this holiday is called Passover, or *Pesah*, which means "pass over."

sending you to Pharaoh to bring the Israelites out of Egypt."

MOSES RETURNS TO EGYPT

And so Moses set out to do what God had commanded. He went to the pharaoh and said, "The Lord, God of Israel, says, 'Let My people go.' " Pharaoh replied, "I do not know this Lord, and I will not let the people Israel go."

God said to Moses, "Pharaoh's heart is stubborn. Go to him in the morning, when he is out at the river. Say to him, 'This will show you that the God of Israel is the Lord.' Then strike the river with your rod. The water will turn into blood; the fish will die, and the Egyptians will have nothing to drink."

Everything happened as God had said it would. But still Pharaoh remained stubborn. So God sent another plague upon Egypt: He made thousands of frogs cover the land. Then Pharaoh sent for Moses, saying, "Ask the Lord to take away the frogs, and I will let your people go." But when the frogs had gone, Pharaoh changed his mind and refused to let the Israelites go.

Then God sent more plagues down upon Egypt: insects so thick that they were like dust in the air; swarms of flies; the death of cattle and other animals; sores that spread on the Egyptians' skins; terrible hail; locusts that ate every growing thing; and absolute darkness for three days. Each time Pharaoh promised to let the Israelites go when the plague lifted, and each time he went back on his word.

THE LAST PLAGUE

Then the Lord said to Moses, "I will bring down one more plague upon Pharaoh, and after this one he will let you go. I will kill the first-born of every Egyptian family and of every animal."

At midnight came the tenth plague. The first-born child of every Egyptian, even of Pharaoh himself, lay dead. Pharaoh was stunned. It was still night when he summoned Moses and said, "Now go, you and the Israelites, leave Egypt this very moment!" So the Israelites

snatched up whatever they owned and hurried out of the land. There was no time to allow the dough they had prepared to rise; they took it with them, carrying it on their backs.

The Israelites left Egypt and trudged out into the wilderness. There the hot sun baked their dough into flat, unrisen loaves of bread. Moses said to the people, "God says that we must remember this day when He brought us out of Egypt. Each year at this time we will have a feast to the Lord, and we will not eat any risen bread for seven days."

THE SEA OF REEDS

The people traveled on through the desert. The Lord went ahead to guide them; by day God appeared as a great column of cloud, and by night as a tower of fire. Finally the Israelites reached the Sea of Reeds. But meanwhile, Pharaoh had begun to be sorry that he had released the Israelites. He sent out his mighty army to capture them. The Israelites saw the Egyptian chariots thundering toward them. On the other side was the sea. They were trapped!

Then God said to Moses, "Lift up your rod, and hold it out over the sea." Moses obeyed. Suddenly a strong wind began to blow. It divided the water until dry land appeared in the middle. The Israelites crossed the sea on the dry ground, between two walls of water. Close after them raced the Egyptian army. But as soon as all the Israelites had crossed the sea, Moses stretched his hand out again. The water rushed back, covering the chariots and their riders. The entire Egyptian army was drowned.

Then the Israelites realized that finally they were free. God, Who is very great, had saved them.

A SONG OF THANKS

You can imagine how the Israelites felt when they saw that the Egyptian army had drowned and they were finally free. They were happy and triumphant. They sang a beautiful song to thank God. Here is part of it.

I will sing to the Lord, for He has won gloriously;
The horse and the rider He has thrown into the sea.
The Lord is my strength; He has saved me.
Who is like You, O Lord, among the mighty?
In Your love You lead the people You rescued;
In Your strength You guide them to Your holy home.
You will plant them on Your own mountain.
The Lord will rule for ever and ever!

WORDS IN HEBREW

The word Exodus means "going out." It is a Greek word. In Hebrew, the Exodus is called the "going out from Egypt." We remember this very important event, just as we remember how God "passed over" the houses of the Jews on the night of the tenth plague. Here are the Hebrew words:

יְצִיאַת מִצְרַיִם GOING OUT FROM EGYPT

פֶּסַח PASSOVER

Pesaḥ

The Time
of Telling Passover is observed for either seven or eight days; but we have a special dinner, the "feast to the Lord" that Moses spoke of, only on the first and second nights. It is called a *Seder*, which means "order," and it has that name because everything is done in a certain order.

When Moses explained the Passover festival to the Israelites, he said, "And you shall *tell* your children on that day, 'It is because of what the Lord did for me when I came out of Egypt.'" *Telling* is really the most important part of the Seder, and *Haggadah*—the Hebrew word for "telling"—is the name of the book we use to guide us through the Seder. The Haggadah tells the history of the

73

Jews' exodus from Egypt and also contains stories, prayers, instructions, and songs. It has been changed and added to, bit by bit, over the years. Because it is very important for everyone to understand the Seder, the Haggadah has been translated into many languages so that it can be used by Jews all over the world. In this country we use Haggadot written in both Hebrew and English.

THE SEDER TABLE *Everything is ready: the Seder plate with its symbols, and the matzah, wine, and Haggadot.*

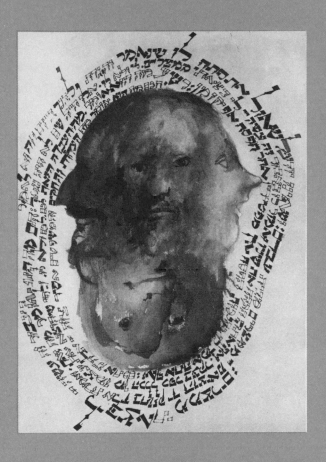

צורת ארבעה בנים דברי תורה

Haggadot

Some Haggadot are beautifully illustrated. A number of illustrated Haggadot–some of them hundreds of years old–are now national treasures displayed in museums. On the left are pages from Haggadot illustrated by two well-known American artists, Leonard Baskin (top) and Ben Shahn (bottom). The picture above, from an old Haggadah, shows the four kinds of people mentioned at the Seder: one who does not know how to ask, one slow to learn, one rebellious, and one wise.

MATZAH AND HAMETZ

Ḥametz means ordinary bread which contains yeast or leavening that makes it rise while it bakes. Ḥametz also means any other food that contains leavening.

Matzah is flat, unrisen bread. It contains no leavening. Matzah is the special Passover food. That is because when the Israelites left Egypt in a great hurry, they carried their half-finished dough on their backs and the sun baked it into flat, unrisen loaves of bread.

Passover is a time different from the rest of the year. It is *Ḥag Hamatzot*, "the feast of unleavened bread." For eight days we eat matzah, and we do not eat any ḥametz.

Eating matzah on the beach at Eilat, in Israel. Eilat is on the shore of the Sea of Reeds. According to tradition, this is where Moses led the Israelites across the sea to safety.

Matzah

This man is preparing matzah according to strict rules which ensure that the dough will not rise.

THE SEDER TABLE

A holiday table is set for the Seder, with a fine tablecloth and special dishes and silver. On one plate are three *matzot*, usually in a beautiful, three-layer cloth *matzah* cover. In the center of the table is set a large platter, the Seder plate; it holds the special Passover symbols, which remind us, in different ways, of our coming out of Egypt:

A roasted shank bone of a lamb (*zeroa*) reminds us of the ancient Jews' sacrifices to God, and of the lambs that were roasted on the night of the first Passover.

A roasted egg (*betzah*) is another reminder of the Temple sacrifices. It also makes us think of spring, the time when eggs hatch and new life begins.

A bitter herb (*maror*), such as horseradish, is so sharp to our tongue that it gives us some idea of the bitterness of slavery.

Haroset is a mixture of chopped apples, chopped nuts, cinnamon, and wine. (In Israel, dates are often used in-

---

GETTING READY FOR PASSOVER

Getting ready for Passover begins before the day itself. The entire house is cleaned. Spring is usually a time for housecleaning, but this cleaning is also to make sure that there are no bits of leavened food (ḥametz) anywhere about. In traditional homes, the family hunt for crumbs with a candle for light and a feather to brush up the crumbs. Then they burn every last trace of ḥametz they have found.

In many homes, there is a special set of dishes and pots which are used only during Passover. That is because our everyday dishes were used with leavened food, but the dishes we eat from on Pesah are special and never touch leaven. Putting away the everyday dishes, and taking the Passover dishes out of storage, is another part of getting ready for Passover.

A wine cup for Elijah.

stead of apples.) It looks like the mortar that holds bricks together, and so it reminds us of the hard labor the Jews were forced to do when they were slaves.

Salt water is like the tears shed by the Israelites during their slavery.

A green vegetable (*karpas*), such as parsley or lettuce, is a symbol of spring, and therefore of hope. We know the world will turn green again after a frozen winter, and in the same way the Jews were brought to freedom after what seemed like a hopeless time of slavery.

Also on the table is a special cup of wine from which no one will drink. It is put there for Elijah the prophet, who we hope will visit us on Pesaḥ night.

ELIJAH

Elijah was a great prophet, a wise man, and a spokesman for God. The Bible tells that Elijah did not die in an ordinary way; instead, he was carried up to heaven in a whirlwind, riding in a fiery chariot. And God promised that someday Elijah would return to the Jews. God said:

I will send you
Elijah the prophet
Before the coming
Of the great day of the Lord.

For hundreds and hundreds of years, Jews have thought of Elijah as their special friend. Jews living in difficult times hoped that Elijah would protect them from dangers that threatened. Each week when Shabbat drew to an end they thought about the worries facing them in the week ahead, and they sang a song asking Elijah to come to them soon. They knew that some day Elijah would return, to tell us that at last a time of peace has come, the "great day of the Lord." Now, when it is time for Havdalah, we too sing *Eliyahu ha-Navi*; we ask Elijah to stand by us through a good week, and bring us to the next peaceful Shabbat.

We celebrate Passover for a number of reasons.

One reason is to *remember*. We never want to forget that we came out of Egypt and out of slavery.

A second reason is to *teach*. Parents tell their children what happened, so that they will be able to tell *their* children.

And a third reason is to *rejoice*. We are very, very glad that we are free people instead of slaves!

The table is set with wine cup and a Haggadah for each person. And on the leader's chair, or sometimes on every person's chair, is a pillow. This is because in ancient times, slaves had to sit on hard benches or even stand during their meals, while free people could lean back on soft sofas. We are free now, and on Seder night we lean on pillows to show the difference between this freedom and our earlier slavery.

This two hundred-year-old Seder plate depicts a Seder meal.

Pesaḥ

Seder
Night
Let's follow the order of the Seder, as it is written in the Haggadah. The Seder begins with the blessing of the candles and then the Kiddush, the blessing over wine. (On Passover, children as well as adults have wine to drink.) Four cups of wine are part of the Seder order.

THE FIRST DIPPING AND THE AFIKOMAN

The leader, after washing his hands, gives each person a piece of the green vegetable to dip into salt water. Everyone says the blessing, thanking God for "the fruit of the earth," before eating. Why do we do this? We are dipping the green vegetable, symbol of spring, life, and hope, into salt water, the symbol of tearful slavery. In this way

80

we combine the very different feelings that Passover brings—on the one hand, hope and happiness, on the other, sadness that our people were once downtrodden and that some Jews still are today.

Next in the Seder comes an exciting moment. The leader takes out the middle matzah of the three and breaks it in half. One half is the *afikoman*, a Greek word that means "dessert." We will need it later on, to share it with all the guests as the last food of the meal. The leader sets it aside now, to save for later. *But* sometime soon, the children will steal the afikoman and hide it. Later, when it is needed, they will receive gifts—either money or presents—in return for the precious afikoman.

The leader uncovers the matzah and explains, "This is the bread of slavery which our ancestors ate in the land of Egypt."

THE FOUR QUESTIONS

Then it is time for the Four Questions. They are asked by the youngest child at the Seder who is able to ask them; sometimes they are asked by all the children present.

Why are the Four Questions so important? Because by asking about various parts of the Seder like the matzah and bitter herbs, you are really asking, "What is the reason for this Passover holiday?" And the answer is that if God had not brought us out of Egypt, we would *still* be slaves. That means that it is not just the Jews of long ago who were set free. *We ourselves* have been set free. That is really important.

Here they are:

1

מַה נִּשְׁתַּנָּה הַלַּיְלָה הַזֶּה מִכָּל־הַלֵּילוֹת.
שֶׁבְּכָל־הַלֵּילוֹת אָנוּ אוֹכְלִין חָמֵץ וּמַצָּה, הַלַּיְלָה הַזֶּה
כֻּלּוֹ מַצָּה.

Ma nish-ta-nah halailah hazeh mikol halaylot? Sheb'chol ha-laylot anu och'lin ḥametz u'matzah, halailah hazeh kulo matzah.

How different this night is from all other nights! On all other nights we eat either bread or matzah; why, tonight, only matzah?

2

שֶׁבְּכָל־הַלֵּילוֹת אָנוּ אוֹכְלִין שְׁאָר יְרָקוֹת, הַלַּיְלָה הַזֶּה מָרוֹר.

Sheb'chol halaylot anu och'lin she'ar ye'rakot halailah hazeh maror.

On all other nights we eat all kinds of vegetables; why, to-night, bitter herbs?

3

שֶׁבְּכָל־הַלֵּילוֹת אֵין אָנוּ מַטְבִּילִין אֲפִלּוּ פַּעַם אֶחָת, הַלַּיְלָה הַזֶּה שְׁתֵּי פְעָמִים.

Sheb'chol halaylot ayn anu matbilin afilu pa-am echat, halailah hazeh·sh'tay fe'amim.

On all other nights, we do not dip our vegetables at all; why, tonight, do we dip them twice?

4

שֶׁבְּכָל־הַלֵּילוֹת אָנוּ אוֹכְלִין בֵּין יוֹשְׁבִין וּבֵין מְסֻבִּין, הַלַּיְלָה הַזֶּה כֻּלָּנוּ מְסֻבִּין.

Sheb'chol halaylot anu och'lin bayn yosh'vin u'vayn me'subin, halailah hazeh kulanu me'subin.

On all other nights, we eat either sitting up or reclining (lean-ing back); why, tonight, do we all recline?

And so—as the leader says in answer to the Four Questions—even if we were all very wise and had studied the Torah a great deal, we would still need to tell the story of the Exodus as we are doing on this night. And now the telling of the Passover story begins.

The Telling

The leader talks about four types of children—one intelligent, one rebellious, one slow to learn, and one shy. Children of all kinds need to hear the Passover story.

Now everyone joins in telling about the story of Exodus.

We list, in song, the many miracles God performed to bring us out of Egypt.

Had God split the Sea of Reeds for us
But not brought us through on dry land
　　—*Dayenu!* (It would have been enough!)
Had He brought us through on dry land
But not helped us in the wilderness
　　—*Dayenu!*

A PASSOVER INVITATION

Before telling the Passover story the leader says, "Let all who are hungry, come and eat; let all who are in need come and celebrate Passover with us." It would be terrible if a Jew could not take part in some Passover Seder. So it is a mitzvah—a duty and a good deed—to keep other Jews in mind on Passover. Through charities we help poorer Jews make a Seder in their homes. And we invite people we know to join us and be our guests on this night. That way no one is left out. And a Seder with plenty of guests is always more fun!

The blessing over wine

The
Seder
Night

"Eating unleavened bread"

84

Reading from the Haggadah

The four questions

Matzah, Bitter Herbs, and Haroset

When the story of the Exodus is over, we are ready to eat matzah. First we make the usual blessing for bread, and then a second, special blessing over the matzah—for the eating of matzah on Pesaḥ was especially commanded by God.

Next each person is given a piece of bitter herb (maror) dipped in ḥaroset to eat. This is the "second dipping" asked about in the Four Questions. It combines two reminders of slavery—a bitter taste and something that looks like mortar for bricks. Then we eat the bitter herb together with the matzah in a "Hillel sandwich," as the great Rabbi Hillel used to do.

The Feast

And now, dinner is served! It is a feast, with many traditional, much-loved foods.

DROPS OF WINE

When we reach the part of the Haggadah that tells of the plagues God brought down on Egypt, it is the custom for each person to spill ten drops of wine—one for each plague. Some people do this by tipping the wine glass over their plates; others by dipping a finger into the wine and then letting the drop fall on the plate. We say the names of the ten plagues as we spill the drops of wine.

Why do we do this? We are glad that God, by bringing the plagues, saved the Jews from slavery. But we are also sorry that the Egyptians had to suffer those plagues. Even though they were our enemies, we are sorry. So this very happy holiday, when we celebrate our freedom, has a little bit of sadness in it. By spilling some of our wine we show that we are taking a little something away from our own holiday pleasure.

The woman in this drawing is making a traditional Passover food—matzah balls.

After dinner comes the dramatic moment when the leader looks for the afikoman he had set aside — and cannot find it! How can it have disappeared? When the children announce that they have the afikoman hidden away, the leader has no choice but to "buy" it back from them with a suitable prize. Then the afikoman is shared among the guests, and the meal is officially over.

COMPLETING THE SEDER

Now comes the time when one of the children opens the door, and we invite the prophet Elijah to join us. For hundreds of years Jews have believed that Elijah will come to announce the arrival of a new age, a time of peace and joy. So each year at Pesah we open the door for Elijah, hoping that this is the year he will come, bringing peace.

We end by asking God to build Jerusalem and keep it strong. The Seder order is completed.

But the evening is not ended. We remain around the table, singing songs. We laugh and talk until it is very late. When we were slaves in Egypt, we could not do this—but now we are free.

WORDS IN HEBREW

At the Passover Seder we read from the Haggadah and eat the special bread called matzah and remove from the house anything that is hametz. Now that you know what all these Hebrew words mean, here is how they look:

סֵדֶר	SEDER
הַגָּדָה	HAGGADAH
מַצָּה	MATZAH
חָמֵץ	HAMETZ

And here are the five things we place on our Seder plate:

זְרוֹעַ	SHANK BONE
בֵּיצָה	EGG
מָרוֹר	BITTER HERB
חֲרֹסֶת	MIXTURE (HAROSET)
כַּרְפַּס	GREEN VEGETABLE

Pesaḥ

Freedom and Springtime

Maybe you are thinking, "It was *thousands* of years ago that the Jews were set free and left Egypt. Why do we still celebrate it all so carefully after such a long time?" It is very hard for us, living in freedom, to imagine that *we ourselves* might have been slaves.

But even long after the Exodus, there have been many, many Jews who were not really free. Jews have often had difficult lives. The Jews were few in number compared to the non-Jews among whom they lived.

THE SONG OF SONGS

On the Shabbat that falls during Passover, we read in the synagogue a book of the Bible called *Shir Hashirim*, the Song of Songs. The Song of Songs is a long poem, a beautiful love poem. Tradition says that it was written by King Solomon to a woman he loved. It may seem very strange for us to read a love poem during Passover. But there is a reason, or, really, two reasons. For one, the Song of Songs is partly about the beauty of nature, about spring:

> Rise up, my love, my fair one, and come away.
> For look, the winter has passed,
> The rain is over and gone;
> The flowers appear on the earth;
> The time of singing has come,
> And the voice of the dove is heard in our land.

Reading these words reminds us that spring is an amazing thing. It makes us grateful to God for making life begin again each year.

There is another reason for reading the Song of Songs. It is a poem about two people who love each other. But it also seems to be about God's love for the Jews and our love for God. It was because of God's special love for us that He freed us from slavery and took us out of Egypt. God chose us and thought of us as most precious, just as the poet who wrote the Song of Songs loved his beloved best of all. She was special, he said. Compared to all the others, she was

> Like a lily among thorns . . .
> Like an apple-tree among the trees of the wood.

And so the Song of Songs brings us back to Passover. It is because of God's love for us that we have the most important things. God gave us the beautiful natural world, and He gave us our freedom. This is what we celebrate in the happy holiday of Passover.

90

Sometimes they were not allowed to attend certain schools, work at certain jobs, own land, or travel. Sometimes they were not even allowed to worship as Jews. At times they worried about their safety, because they knew that their non-Jewish neighbors might attack them and would not be punished.

LONGING FOR FREEDOM

When Jews, through the centuries, celebrated Passover, their feelings about the holiday were not the same as ours. They thanked God for freeing them from the Egyptians; but they still longed for complete freedom. When they said *Leshanah habaah birushalayim*, "Next year in Jerusalem," and when they waited for Elijah, they were dreaming about a life of peace and happiness that would be entirely different from their real lives. Like us, they leaned back on pillows to show that they were free people. But for them it was only on this Passover night, in their own homes, that they could be really free. They knew that in their everyday lives they would suffer scorn and mistreatment.

Today, we are lucky to be living as Jews in lands of freedom. But there are still many Jews living in certain lands, especially the Soviet Union (Russia), who are made to suffer terribly because they are Jewish. We think of them especially when we celebrate this holiday of freedom. Some families have a special "fourth matzah" as part of their Seder, to remember the Jews of Russia, who are still, in a way, living in slavery.

THE SPRING FESTIVAL

Pesaḥ is a double holiday. We have seen that it is a holiday of freedom. But it is also a holiday of springtime. Long, long ago, even before they were in Egypt, Jews celebrated the coming of spring. They rejoiced that life had begun again, that their crops were growing and their cattle giving birth. They thanked God by offering grain and by roasting and feasting on a young lamb. This feast took place on the 15th of Nisan (which is the first spring month). That is the very date on which the exodus from Egypt began. The Israelites used the blood of the spring lambs they had sacrificed to mark the doorposts of their houses on Passover night. And it is still the 15th of Nisan on which we begin the celebration of Passover.

COUNTING THE OMER

Pesaḥ comes at the time when, in biblical days, the first crop of barley was harvested. On the second day of Pesaḥ, a bundle, or *Omer*, of barley was brought to the Temple as a gift to God. And every day after that, for seven weeks (or 49 days), the "Omer" was counted in the Temple. On the 50th day the second spring crop would be ready to harvest. By bringing the bundles of barley to God, the Israelites were asking God to send rain and to make this second crop a good one. The 50th day is also the date of Shavuot. Although we do not bring barley to the Temple anymore, Jews still "count the Omer," 50 days that start on the second day of Passover and end at Shavuot.

WORDS IN HEBREW

Pesaḥ is known in Hebrew by three other names. Each tells a part of the Passover story. Here they are:

חַג הַמַּצּוֹת	FESTIVAL OF (EATING) MATZAH
חַג הָאָבִיב	FESTIVAL OF SPRING
זְמַן חֵרוּתֵנוּ	SEASON OF OUR FREEDOM

In ancient times, a sheaf—or bundle—of barley was brought to the Temple as an offering on the second day of Passover. Then the Israelites counted 49 days from the time of this offering. The sheaf was called an Omer; and the 49 days of waiting was called the Counting of the Omer.

עֹמֶר	SHEAF
סְפִירַת הָעֹמֶר	COUNTING OF THE OMER

Shavuot

The Festival of Weeks

Shavuot means "weeks." Since Passover we have been counting the Omer for 49 days, or seven weeks; finally we reach Shavuot, the "festival of weeks." Those seven weeks have brought us all the way through the springtime. On Pesaḥ we welcomed the beginning of spring, and now on Shavuot we celebrate the beginning of summer.

SHAVUOT IN ANCIENT TIMES

Because the ancient Israelites were farmers, Shavuot, like other holidays, is closely tied to the cycle of growing things. Shavuot celebrates the year's first harvest. Farmers could feel now, with relief, that they had come through the anxious days of the Omer and had begun to reap a good harvest. To thank God, they brought harvest offerings. In thanks for the ripened wheat, two fine loaves of bread were offered in the Temple. Another offering was made of "first fruits." The Talmud tells us that when a farmer saw an especially beautiful fruit ripening on one of his trees, he tied a ribbon around its stem, to set it aside as an offering. On Shavuot the farmer filled a basket with these perfect fruits, to bring to the Temple.

All across the ancient land of Israel, farm families joined the processions bound for Jerusalem. They carried harvest branches and their baskets of offerings. Musicians playing instruments accompanied these pilgrimage "parades." Finally they reached Jerusalem, where they were joyfully greeted by the townspeople. The procession continued up the hill to the Temple; there each family presented its basket of fruits. It was a happy, exciting, festive day.

We do not offer crops to God any more, but on Shavuot we decorate the synagogue, and our homes, with branches and fruits.

THE FESTIVAL OF THE TORAH

Like many other Jewish holidays, Shavuot is a double holiday. One part of it has to do with the cycle of nature: it is a harvest festival. But another side of this holiday has to do with the story of the Jews. Shavuot is the anniversary of the day when the Israelites at Mount Sinai received the

Israeli children gather
"fruits of the field."

First
Fruits

Bringing grain from the
first harvest.

Ten Commandments, a sign of our covenant, or *berit*, from God. That is certainly one of the most important events in our whole history. The Torah tells us who we are, and it tells us how to live. It tells us—in the Ten Commandments, and in other places—what is right and what is wrong. We need the Torah just as much as we need the food grown by farmers, and so on Shavuot we have quite a lot to be thankful for.

In many religious schools, Shavuot is the time when the older students are "confirmed" or graduated. Confirmation or graduation shows that a whole course of study has been completed. It also means that these students are taking their places as grown members of the Jewish community. So, in a way, it is the celebration of another kind of harvest: these students are ready to offer the "first fruits" of their studies, and on Shavuot we celebrate their study of Torah and its commandments.

OBSERVING SHAVUOT

On Shavuot eve, traditional Jews observe the custom of staying up all night in the synagogue, reading Torah and studying together. (An old legend says that on this night the heavens open, so prayers will have an especially good chance of rising up to reach God.)

The next morning, as part of the Shavuot service, the portion of the Torah is read that describes God's giving the Torah on Mount Sinai. We read the Ten Commandments and sing songs of praise to God. We also read another part of the Bible, the Book of Ruth—a beautiful story which took place at harvest time.

On Shavuot it is the custom to eat foods made with grains and with milk products—for instance, blintzes or cheese cake. One reason for this is our idea of the Torah as "milk and honey," the perfect, sweetest foods.

In Israel, parades are sometimes held on Shavuot. Children carry decorated baskets of fruit, to remind us of the offerings of "first fruits" made by the Israelites so long ago. One name for Shavuot is *Hag Ḥabikkurim*, the Festival of the First Fruits.

WORDS IN HEBREW

In this chapter we learned two names for Shavuot. This is how they look in Hebrew:

שָׁבוּעוֹת   WEEKS (SHAVUOT)

חַג הַבְּכוּרִים   FESTIVAL OF THE FIRST FRUITS

Shavuot

The Story
of Ruth The part of the Bible called The Book of Ruth tells a beautiful story that we always read on Shavuot.

Long ago in ancient Israel there lived a man named Elimelech, his wife, Naomi, and their two sons. But in Israel there was a long famine, a time of hunger. So Elimelech and his family went to live in the land of Moab. There the sons grew up and married two non-Jewish, Moabite girls named Orpah and Ruth.

After some years both Elimelech and his sons died. Naomi and her two daughters-in-law were left alone.

99

Naomi decided to return to her old home, to Israel. She said to Ruth and Orpah, "Go back to your mothers' houses. I hope that you will each find a new husband and have a good life."

RUTH AND NAOMI

Orpah kissed Naomi good-bye and left her. But Ruth said, "I will not leave you. Wherever you go, I will go; where you live, I will live. Your people shall be my people, and your God shall be my God." Naomi saw that Ruth's mind was made up. So Naomi and Ruth journeyed back to Israel together and went to live in Naomi's old home, the city of Bethlehem.

Naomi and Ruth were poor. It was spring, the time of the barley harvest. In those days, poor people were allowed to glean—to gather leftover stalks of grain—after the farm workers had finished reaping the harvest. So Ruth went to glean barley after the reapers.

RUTH AND BOAZ

While Ruth was gathering grain, the owner of the field where she worked came to inspect his crops. He was a wealthy man named Boaz. Ruth was beautiful, and Boaz noticed her among the other gleaners. "Who is that maiden?" he asked his helper. "She is a Moabite woman who came back from Moab with Naomi," the helper replied.

Now it happened that Boaz was a cousin of Naomi's. He had heard about this faithful young woman who had left her own people and her own land in order to stay with

Naomi and become a Jewess. So Boaz said to Ruth, "You can glean in my field throughout the harvest. When you are thirsty, drink the water that my workers have drawn, and when you are hungry, eat with my reapers. No one will hurt you." Ruth bowed and said, "You are very kind to show such concern, for I am only a foreigner."

Then Boaz went to his reapers and said, "Let that young woman glean anywhere she likes, even among the bound sheaves. And pull some more barley out of the bundles and leave it for her, and let her take as much as she can." So Ruth gleaned all day in the field, and every day after that, for the rest of the barley and wheat harvests.

RUTH FINDS A NEW HUSBAND

One day Naomi said to Ruth, "My daughter, I ought to find you a husband and a home, so you can be happy. And Boaz is a kinsman of ours, a cousin. Tonight he will be separating the barley from the stalks, working on the threshing floor. Put on your best clothes, and go there. When he has finished and lies down to sleep, go uncover his feet, and lie at his feet. Then he will know you are asking for his protection."

Ruth did as her mother-in-law had instructed. She went to the threshing floor and watched, without being seen. When Boaz had eaten and was full of good spirits, he lay down on a bed of straw to sleep. Ruth came softly in the dark, and uncovered his feet, and lay down there. At midnight Boaz was startled in his sleep. He sat up, and there was a woman, lying at his feet. "Who are you?" he asked. "I am your servant, Ruth," she replied. "Give me your protection, for you are my near kinsman."

Then Boaz said, "Do not be afraid. I will protect you. I will marry you."

Boaz and Ruth were happily married. They had a son named Obed.

When Obed grew up he had a son named Jesse, and in time Jesse had a son named David. And David became king over all Israel.

RUTH AND THE JEWS

The story of Ruth shows something important. Ruth is a very honored person, because she was the great-grandmother of King David. She is a *matriarch*, one of the "mothers" of the Jewish people. And Ruth was not even a Jew by birth! It did not matter that she had not been born Jewish; what mattered was that she was kind and generous. Ruth was a convert to Judaism. She lived according to the laws of the Torah. So now we know another reason, beside the harvest theme, for reading the story of Ruth on Shavuot.

Shavuot

The Precious
Gift
Shavuot is the anniversary of one of the most important happenings in the whole long history of the Jews—the giving of the Torah.

Moses had freed the Jews from Pharaoh and led them out of Egypt and safely across the Sea of Reeds. Now they were wandering in the wilderness. After many days they came to the foot of Mount Sinai.

Then God called out of the mountain to the Israelites. God said, "You have seen how I rescued you from the Egyptians. Now, if you will listen to My promise and keep My agreement, then you will be My treasure among all the peoples. All people on the earth are Mine, but you will be a holy nation to Me."

103

The Ten Commandments

1. *I am the Lord your God, Who brought you out of the land of Egypt. Do not worship any other gods.*

2. *Do not worship idols.*

3. *Do not swear falsely by the name of the Lord your God.*

4. *Remember the Sabbath day and keep it holy.*

5. *Honor your father and mother.*

6. *Do not murder.*

7. *Do not commit adultery.*

8. *Do not steal.*

9. *Do not bear false witness against another person.*

10. *Do not wish to own what another person already owns.*

The Israelites all answered together, "Everything that the Lord has said we will do."

On the morning of the third day, the people heard thunder and saw lightning and a thick cloud on the top of Mount Sinai. Trembling, they gathered at the foot of the mountain. From flame and smoke on the mountain top came the loud sound of the shofar. Then the people heard the voice of God.

God said, "I am the Lord your God, Who brought you out of the land of Egypt, out of slavery. Do not worship any other gods."

Then God taught the people His commandments, which we call the Ten Commandments.

The people were afraid when they heard the voice of God. But Moses said, "Do not be afraid; the Lord has spoken to you so that you will really believe Him and keep His commandments."

Then Moses went up onto the mountain. There he wrote the Ten Commandments on two tablets of stone. And there God told him many other things that the Israelites needed to know. All of God's instructions to the Israelites are in the Torah. The Torah tells us how we should act in order to live good, honorable lives.

BERIT OR COVENANT

God made this offer to the Jews. God would give us the commandments—Torah. If we agreed to follow the commandments, we would be God's special people. The Israelites accepted God's agreement. We call it our covenant or Berit.

And so, from that day onward, the Jews began to live in a special way, *as Jews*, according to God's Torah.

Shavuot dancing during an all-night prayer service.

Celebrating
Shavuot

A sunrise service.

Outdoor services held at a camp in California.

This kiddush cup is especially made for Shavuot.

FREEDOM AND TORAH

There is a strong connection between Pesaḥ, when the Jews were given their *freedom*, and Shavuot, when they were given the *Torah*. Remember that we count the days between Passover—the anniversary of our freedom—and Shavuot. That is not just because of the harvest, but also because freedom and Torah go together. God gave the Israelites their freedom. But to be free without having any idea of how to live is to be like an animal. If we are going to live *well*, to live lives that we are proud of, then we need to know what is right and what is wrong. We need rules to help us do the things that are kind and fair and to show us which things are mean or cruel. These rules, that we got from God, are a precious gift. God's law is as precious as freedom.

On Shavuot we celebrate, in a way, the good things that happen when God and people work together. God gives us the natural world, and we farm it carefully: the result is a full harvest. God gives us laws of what is right and wrong, and we do our best to live by them: the result is a stronger, better, happier world.

People used to ask a famous rabbi, "Why is Shavuot called the festival of the *giving* of our Torah, not of the *receiving* of the Torah?" The rabbi answered, "The *giving* of the Torah was on Shavuot. The *receiving* must happen every day of the year."

Some religions are built around what their members believe. But for Jews, how we *live* is fully as important as what we *believe*. That is why the Torah, which is the center of Judaism, is *not* something we worship. It is something we live by. It is not something for God; it is something for *us*, for us to use every day of the year.

WORDS IN HEBREW

Shavuot is called the Festival of the First Fruits, which reminds us that it was celebrated in ancient times as a farm festival. It is called Weeks or Shavuot to remind us that we have counted seven weeks of seven days (49 days) since the time of the Omer on Passover. But it has a third name which reminds us of the special gift we celebrate on this holiday:

זְמַן מַתַּן תּוֹרָתֵנוּ   SEASON OF THE GIVING OF OUR TORAH

Holidays and History

Some holidays began after the time of the Torah. These minor holidays were not commanded by God. They are celebrations of victories and of happy—or sometimes, sad—events which are part of the history of the Jewish people. We can read about some of these events in books of the Bible that come after the Torah. These holidays, and the history they are based on, were also written about by the rabbis in later times.

Ḥanukkah

Bravery and Miracles

Ḥanukkah. It is a holiday of fun and parties, of secrets and presents, of candle-lighting for eight exciting nights. We look forward to Ḥanukkah throughout the year. With all the excitement, it is sometimes even hard to remember the reason for celebrating Ḥanukkah.

Of course, we know about Judah Maccabee and the oil that burned for eight nights. But now we will look a little closer at the story of Ḥanukkah, because it is very interesting. And it is true.

112

GREEK WAYS AND GREEK GODS

In ancient days a Greek general, Alexander the Great, conquered all the lands around the Mediterranean Sea. Alexander and the emperors that followed him made sure that the Greek way of life was brought to all these faraway places. And so, everywhere, people learned to speak the Greek language; to wear Greek clothes; to take Greek names; to spend a great deal of time on sports, as the Greeks did; to read Greek books; and to worship Greek gods.

In Judea (all that was left of the ancient kingdom of Israel), some Jews liked the idea of "becoming Greek." Of course they knew they were still Jews, but they admired Greek customs and wanted to follow them. It made them feel they were "in fashion," to be like the Greeks—the rulers of the world.

There were many other Jews who did not want to follow the ways of the Greeks. They went on living and worshiping in Jewish ways. But King Antiochus of Syria, who became the ruler of Judea, decided to destroy the Jewish religion completely. He set altars to the Greek idols in every town and ordered all Jews to worship the Greek gods. Anyone caught studying or teaching the Torah or even keeping the Sabbath would be put to death.

MATTATHIAS THE PRIEST

In the little town of Modin, an old priest named Mattathias refused to worship the Greek gods. One day when a Jew came up to the altar to sacrifice to a statue of the Greek god Zeus, Mattathias grew so furious that he struck

113

Many Shapes For The Menorah

A Hannukah menorah can be shaped in many ways. Often it looks like a traditional seven-branched menorah, but with four branches on each side instead of three. Sometimes it has all the candle holders in a row. Because the menorah can have so many different shapes, it has been a favorite holy object for sculptors and artists to make.

This menorah sits atop the water tower of a kibbutz in Israel.

The world's largest menorah being set up in New York City.

A silver menorah made in the 19th century.

The Syrian armies were not worried when they first began to have trouble fighting the Maccabees. They knew that on the Sabbath Jews are not permitted to work—or to fight. "We will attack them on the Sabbath and destroy the whole Jewish army," they told each other. But Mattathias and the Maccabees decided that it was even more important to save Jewish lives than to keep Shabbat. So when the Syrians attacked them on the Sabbath, they fought back as strongly as ever. Soon, the Syrians began to worry.

the Jew and killed him. Then he attacked the king's soldiers who were standing guard.

Mattathias knew that his life was now in danger. He fled with his five sons into the mountains. "Let all those who want to obey the Torah and keep the Commandments follow me," he said. Some brave Jews joined Mattathias. This little group became an army that hid in the mountains and attacked the Syrians whenever they could.

JUDAH MACCABEE

Before long, Mattathias died. His son Judah, "the Maccabee," became leader of the band. Under Judah, this small Jewish army grew powerful. They knew the rocky mountains of their own country better than the Syrian army did: time and again they would trap the Syrian soldiers in narrow mountain passes, then attack and defeat them. And they knew how to hide in the mountains so the enemy could not find them.

For three years the Maccabees fought on. Bit by bit they forced the mighty Syrian army farther and farther back. Finally they staged a surprise attack on Jerusalem

The mighty Syrian army used 32 huge elephants to strengthen one of their attacks against the Maccabees. Each elephant carried a tower-like shelter on its back, from which soldiers could throw spears or fire arrows. It was like a living tank. One of Judah's brothers, Eleazar, saw an elephant with royal decorations on its armor. He knew that the Syrian king or one of his most important generals must be riding on that elephant. Eleazar fought his way right up to the elephant, then slipped beneath it where there was no armor, stabbed it in the stomach, and killed it. The elephant fell on Eleazar and crushed him; at the same time the tower crashed to the ground and the men inside it died in battle. Brave Eleazar had given his life to help the Maccabees with the war.

and drove off the Syrian troops. They had taken Israel's capital from the enemy; they had won!

Cleansing the Temple

Judah and his triumphant army marched to the Temple. They ripped down the huge statue of Zeus that stood above the altar. And then, although they were tired from hard fighting, they began to clean the Temple. They cleared away everything used for Greek worship. They scrubbed and polished and brought back the Torah and all the holy objects.

Now they were ready to dedicate the Temple again, to proclaim that it was again a house for the worship of the One God. It was time to light the great lamp, the *menorah*, which would burn on and on and would never be allowed to die.

The Temple was rededicated that very night. The Hebrew word for dedication is *Ḥanukkah*. This was the first Ḥanukkah.

THE MIRACLE OF THE OIL

A legend tells that Judah and his followers could not find enough holy oil to keep the menorah burning. Only one tiny bottle of oil was left in the storerooms, enough to last about one day. Judah sent for more oil, but he knew it would take many days to arrive, for the oil had to be pressed from olives that grew in the north.

Then, a miracle happened. Although there was hardly any oil in the menorah, its light did not go out. On it burned—two nights, three nights, four nights—eight nights in all. By that time, new oil had arrived. The menorah was refilled and continued to burn. Not once had its light died.

And so at Ḥanukkah, we have many thing to celebrate. We celebrate the rededication of the Temple. We celebrate the story of the miracle by which a tiny flame burned on and on, and the other miracle by which a tiny band of brave Jews saved our religion.

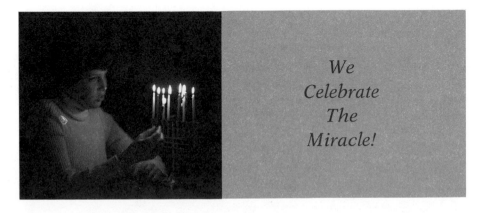

*We
Celebrate
The
Miracle!*

The war that Judah and the Maccabees fought was a war for religious freedom. They were ruled by an emperor who might punish them by death, just for praying to God.

There have been many people who had to struggle for religious freedom. Most of the early settlers in America, both Jews and Christians, came here to escape from countries where they could be harshly punished just for praying according to their beliefs.

WORDS IN HEBREW

In this chapter you learned about three Hebrew words. One is the name of our holiday, a name that reminds us of the reason for the holiday. One is the special lamp that we use to celebrate the holiday. And one is the name that was given to Judah, the son of Mattathias, who led the small Jewish army to victory.

חֲנֻכָּה	DEDICATION
מְנוֹרָה	LAMP, OR CANDELABRA
מַכַּבִּ"י	MACCABEE

Some say that the name Maccabee comes from the Hebrew word for "hammer." But some say that it comes from the first letters of the first four words of a Hebrew prayer.

מִי כָמֹכָה בָּאֵלִים, יְיָ?	WHO IS LIKE YOU AMONG THE GODS, O LORD?

118

Ḥanukkah

It's Ḥanukkah! The first night of Ḥanukkah arrives at last. The house is hung with decorations—paper chains, stars of David, paper candles, and *dreidels*. Now it is time to light the menorah.

The Ḥanukkah menorah is a special candle holder, used only at Ḥanukkah. It is also called a Ḥanukkiah. It has spaces for eight candles, which stand for the eight nights that the oil burned on the first Ḥanukkah. And it has a separate place for a ninth candle. The *Shammash*. Shammash means "servant"; we use the Shammash to light the other candles.

119

PLAYING DREIDEL

HOW TO PLAY DREIDEL

Each person starts the game with a supply of counters—raisins, nuts, or pennies. There is also a pile of counters in the center, the "pot." The players take turns spinning the dreidel and then following its directions. The letter that lands facing up on the dreidel tells the player what to do with the counters. A good way to remember is:

נ nun = "none"; player gets nothing.
ג gimel = "get"; player takes everything in the pot.
ה hay = "half"; player takes half of what is in the pot.
ש shin = "share"; each player must put counters in the pot.

When all but one person is out of counters, the game is over. The player with all the counters wins!

120

Here are the blessings over the candles:

בָּרוּךְ אַתָּה, יְיָ אֱלֹהֵינוּ, מֶלֶךְ הָעוֹלָם, אֲשֶׁר קִדְּשָׁנוּ בְּמִצְוֹתָיו וְצִוָּנוּ לְהַדְלִיק נֵר שֶׁל חֲנֻכָּה.

Baruch atah adonai elohenu melech ha-olam asher kidshanu b'mitzvotav v'tzivanu l'hadlik ner shel ḥanukkah.

Blessed are You, Lord our God, King of the Universe, Who blessed us with the commandments and commanded us to kindle the Ḥanukkah lights.

בָּרוּךְ אַתָּה, יְיָ אֱלֹהֵינוּ, מֶלֶךְ הָעוֹלָם, שֶׁעָשָׂה נִסִּים לַאֲבוֹתֵינוּ בַּיָּמִים הָהֵם בַּזְּמַן הַזֶּה.

Baruch atah adonai elohenu melech ha-olam she'asah nisim la-avotaynu ba-yamin ha-hem bazman hazeh.

Blessed are You, Lord our God, King of the Universe, Who worked miracles for our ancestors in long-ago days, at this season.

On the first night of Ḥanukkah, a third blessing is also said:

בָּרוּךְ אַתָּה, יְיָ אֱלֹהֵינוּ, מֶלֶךְ הָעוֹלָם, שֶׁהֶחֱיָנוּ וְקִיְּמָנוּ וְהִגִּיעָנוּ לַזְּמַן הַזֶּה.

Baruch atah adonai elohenu melech ha-olam sheheheyanu v'kiye manu v'hi-gi-anu lazman hazeh.

Blessed are You, Lord our God, King of the universe, Who has kept us alive and strong and brought us to this season.

LIGHTING THE CANDLES

On the first night of Ḥanukkah we set one candle in the menorah, on the right-hand side, and we also put in the Shammash.

As soon as it is dark, it is time to light the menorah. The family gathers around. There is at least one menorah to light; but it is even better if there are several, or one for each member of the family.

First we light the Shammash with a match. Then, holding the Shammash, we sing the blessings. One is a blessing over the candles. The second thanks God for performing the Ḥanukkah miracles that saved our religion. A third blessing, which we say only on the first night, thanks God for bringing us to this happy moment.

We light the candle and put the Shammash back in its holder. Then we put the menorah in the window, or in another place where it is sure to be seen.

Ḥanukkah Games

Now it is time for fun and games. Many songs are traditional at Ḥanukkah. *Ma'oz Tzur*, Rock of Ages, tells how time after time God saved the Jewish people. Other songs tell of the bravery of Judah Maccabee, or the beauty of the menorah lights, or—of course—the little dreidel made of clay. Some songs are fun to dance to or act out: you can spin like a dreidel, battle like the Maccabees, or take turns pretending to "light" one another like candles lined up in a menorah. Ḥanukkah is a holiday for all kinds of fun.

You can play many games at Ḥanukkah, but the traditional one is spinning the *dreidel*. A dreidel is a little top with four sides. On each side is a different Hebrew letter: *nun*, *gimel*, *hay*, and *shin*. They are the first letters of a

122

Hebrew sentence, *Nes Gadol Hayah Sham*, which means "A great miracle happened there."

Hanukkah is a good time to have a party. Besides singing songs and playing games, you might like to dance Jewish and Israeli dances, like the *horah*. And for refreshments, you can serve special Hanukkah foods. We eat foods fried in oil at Hanukkah, because they remind us of the miraculous little bottle of oil. *Latkes* are fried pancakes made of potato. In Israel it is the custom to serve little jelly donuts, *sufganiot*, which are also fried in oil. (They taste just as good outside of Israel!)

Hanukkah Gifts

One more Hanukkah custom that everyone likes is giving gifts. It is a rather old tradition to give children money, or Hanukkah *gelt*. Exchanging presents is a newer custom.

We continue to celebrate Hanukkah (although probably not with parties!) for eight nights. On the second night we place two candles on the right side of the menorah, sing the blessings, and kindle the candles with the Shammash. Night after night the number of candles grows, until on the eighth night the menorah stands filled and triumphant!

We have had eight happy, exciting Hanukkah days. Now, as we watch the row of blazing candles, we might be remembering the words of a Hanukkah song: "One for each night, they shed a great light, to remind us of days long ago."

THE SHOW IS ON!

The Ḥanukkah story is so exciting that it makes a wonderful play. You can make up a play and perform it at home or in school. If your group is small, each child can take several parts. Here are some suggestions for the roles in your play:

Mattathias
Antiochus, King of Syria
Judah
Maccabees
Eleazar
Syrian soldiers
Menorah lights

You might want to make cardboard swords and shields for the battle scenes. Perhaps your parents will lend you some cups, bowls, or candlesticks to use as holy objects in the Temple.

WORDS IN HEBREW

Playing dreidel is a good way of remembering what Ḥanukkah is all about. The four letters on the sides of the dreidel are the first letters of four words that say a great deal about this holiday.

נֵס גָּדוֹל הָיָה שָׁם   A GREAT MIRACLE HAPPENED THERE.

And, just for fun, you might want to learn the word for Israel's favorite Ḥanukkah food, jelly donuts. (Here we eat potato pancakes, called latkes in Yiddish.)

סֻפְגָּנִיּוֹת   JELLY DONUTS

124

Ḥanukkah

Festival of Lights

When we think of Ḥanukkah we think of shining lights. We light candles on Ḥanukkah to remind us of the miraculous oil that burned for eight days, on the first Ḥanukkah. But there is also another reason, a very interesting one.

Long ago, long before the time of the Maccabees, the Jews had a mid-winter festival on which they lit flames. They were celebrating because the time of long nights was ending; soon the *days* would begin to grow longer again, soon spring would return.

In fact, all people from the very earliest times have celebrated the turn of winter in some way. To people in ancient times, winter was hard and darkness was frightening. When they saw the sun's rays growing weaker and shining for a shorter time each day, they were afraid that the sun might disappear entirely and be lost to them forever. And so, when the days stopped getting shorter and began instead to grow longer—this usually happens around December 21 on our calendar and is called the winter solstice—people rejoiced. They believed that light, which gives life, had triumphed over fearful darkness.

As people learned more about the world, they realized there was no need to be afraid of darkness. But they still joyfully celebrated the winter solstice, the time when light returns. The ancient Jews had such a festival.

THE FIRST MENORAH

A Ḥanukkah menorah has nine branches or candle holders—one for each night of the holiday and one for the Shammash candle.

A menorah with seven branches is an even older symbol of Judaism. The Torah contains God's instructions for making all the holy objects used in the Ancient Temple. Among them was a lamp, or menorah, to be beaten out of pure gold. It should have three branches on each side, God said, and one in the center, and decorations shaped like almond blossoms.

The menorah that was made according to God's instructions stood in the Temple in Jerusalem. It was this lamp that the Maccabees restored when they cleansed the Temple, and in which the miraculous oil burned for eight nights. The idea of a Ḥanukkah menorah is based on the Temple menorah, but with two branches added, making nine altogether.

126

FESTIVAL OF LIGHT *Lighting the candles reminds us of the miraculous oil that burned for eight days.*

Later came the great victory of the Maccabees. The Temple was rededicated on the 25th of the month of Kislev, which is right around the time of the winter solstice. It was natural for Ḥanukkah to be combined with the earlier holiday, and to become the "festival of lights."

The story about the miraculous oil burning for eight nights may be a legend that was added on to the true story of the Maccabees' heroic victory. But the two stories really seem to belong together. One is about a tiny light that, by the strength of a miracle, triumphed over dark-

Bringing Light To The Darkness

Jews in all parts of the world celebrate Ḥannukkah. Here are candles being lit in Israel, Bucharia, Pakistan, and the United States.

ness. The other is about a small people who, with courage and belief in God, triumphed over a powerful enemy trying to destroy them. We could say that they kept the light of Judaism burning, against the darkness.

HILLEL AND SHAMMAI

When Ḥanukkah was still a rather new holiday, there was a difference of opinion on how it should be celebrated. The students of one rabbi, Shammai, said that Ḥanukkah should begin with eight lights, and one should be taken away each night. But the followers of Hillel said that, on the contrary, Ḥanukkah should begin with one light, and one should be *added* each night, because "holiness is something that must grow, not become smaller." Ever since then we have celebrated Hillel's way, because the growing number of Ḥanukkah lights matches our feeling

BEING PROUD

The events of Ḥanukkah, although they happened long ago, can tell us quite a lot about our own lives. The Jews were living in the middle of a Greek world—just as we today live in a Christian country. Some Jews liked the Greek customs and wanted to act as if they, too, were Greek. They wanted to be like everybody else. But other Jews, for whom the Maccabees fought, wanted to be Jews, not Greeks. Though they were few in number, they were proud of their Jewishness. They cared so much about keeping their religion that they were even willing to die for it, if necesary.

We are lucky. We do not have to fight for the right to be Jews. But we are, like the ancient Israelites, a small group surrounded by many, many people who are different from us. We are proud of being Jews. If we push aside our Jewishness and try to act like the people around us, we will not feel proud to be ourselves anymore. Like the Maccabees, we need to stand up for what we believe.

129

of growing pride in the history of Ḥanukkah, and our joy that the world is turning toward the season of light.

And so at Ḥanukkah, as each night you kindle another shining light in your menorah, you will know that you are doing something that was very important to people thousands of years ago; something that the Maccabees and their followers risked their lives to do; and something that still today has very special meaning to us, as Jews.

This "Ḥanukkiyah" is made of tin.

NAMES AND THINGS

We usually use the word menorah to speak of the special candle holder used at Ḥanukkah. But "menorah" is really just the Hebrew word for any kind of lamp or lighting fixture. In Israel, the word refers to *any* lamp—even an electric one. So a different word, *Ḥanukkiyah*, is used to describe a Ḥanukkah candle holder.

CANDLES OR OIL?

In biblical days, people did not have candles. Their lamps had a cuplike space to contain oil (they probably used olive oil). A wick was put into the oil, and the end of the wick was lighted. Candles are cleaner and less trouble, and that is why we use them today; but there is no reason why we could not use an oil-burning menorah at Ḥanukkah, to help us imagine more completely the time of the Maccabees.

MAKE YOUR OWN

One of the best ways to enjoy Ḥanukkah is to make your own menorah. Clay is a good material for this, although you can also use wood if you are careful about watching the candles burn down. You can drill holes or glue spools or metal nuts onto a piece of wood. Check the size of the holes against the type of candle you plan to use. Or, make a clay oil-burning menorah, with nine hollows to contain the oil, and nine small lips to hold the wicks.

WORDS IN HEBREW

Another name for Ḥanukkah shows how important light is on this winter holiday. It's so important that we even use a special light, the *Shammash* candle, to kindle all the other lights. Here are three Hebrew words for Ḥanukkah:

שַׁמָּשׁ	SHAMMASH, THE "SERVANT" CANDLE
נֵרוֹת חֲנֻכָּה	HANUKKAH CANDLES
חַג הָאוּרִים	FESTIVAL OF LIGHTS

131

Tu bi-Shevat

The Birthday of the Trees

Tu bi-Shevat means "the 15th day of the month of Shevat." This is the day when we celebrate the New Year of the Trees.

In biblical times, Jews brought fruit from their trees as an offering to God. The Torah says: for the first three years after a tree has been planted you may not eat its fruit. The fourth year (this is the first good year), offer the fruit to God in praise and thanks. On the fifth year, and after that, you may eat the fruit of your tree.

Of course, it is difficult to keep track of the exact day when each tree was planted. So the rabbis assigned a

132

special day, the 15th of Shevat, to be the "birthday" of all trees. On that day every tree was counted as a year older.

In Israel, this date comes at the time when the trees do seem to be "born"—to come to life. The winter rains are ending, the air is turning warm. Sap rises in the trees, and green buds appear. The whole world feels new; this really is a kind of "new year." And so, for a very long time, Tu bi-Shevat has been a day not just for counting but for rejoicing.

TREES AND THE LAND

The fact that trees have a new year all to themselves shows how important trees have always been to the Jews. In a hot, dry country like Israel, trees make the difference between an unfriendly desert and a good land. The roots

THINKING AHEAD

A story is told about an old man who was planting a carob tree in his garden when the king happened to ride by. "Old man, is that a tree you are planting?" inquired the king.
"Yes, your majesty, a carob tree."
"And how long will it be before your carob tree bears fruit?"
"About seventy years."
"Seventy years!" laughed the king. "Why do you bother to plant this tree, since you will not live to eat its fruit?"
"I have often eaten carob from trees planted before *my* time," replied the old man. "Years from now, after I am gone, my grandchildren will be able to eat the fruit of this tree."
The old man knew something that the king did not: when we plant a tree we show our love for the world, and we help to make it a better place.

Planting
Trees
In Israel

of trees hold moisture in the soil, helping many plants to grow. Trees provide shade, and fruits for food, and wood for fuel and for building.

The Jews of ancient Israel knew how much they depended on trees. They knew that they must plant new trees so that the land would go on being green and rich. So Tu bi-Shevat became a special day for planting trees. It was the custom to plant a young cedar tree for every boy born during the year and a young cypress for every girl. In this way the beginning of life was celebrated by the beginning of more life. When a grown boy and girl were married, cedar branches from his tree and cypress branches from hers were woven together to form a *ḥupah*, or marriage canopy.

In later times, most Jews lived outside of Israel. They often lived in cooler climates where trees grew in such numbers that they were taken for granted. But Jews still remembered that the 15th of Shevat is the new year of the trees and celebrated the day by eating foods that grow on the trees of the Holy Land—almonds, dates, figs, carob, and pomegranates.

MAKING THE DESERT BLOOM AGAIN

Today our people live again in the land of Israel, and trees are just as important there as they were in biblical times. When Jews resettled Israel in modern times they found that through neglect much of the land had become bare desert or swampy marsh. By planting and caring for millions of trees they have turned Israel back into a green and blooming land.

Tu Bi-Shevat
In
Israel

Children of all ages—from kindergarten to high school—plant trees in the fields, and on the hills.

For us Tu bi-Shevat is a winter day, but we can still celebrate the birthday of the trees by planting trees—in Israel. Each year on this day Jews from all over the world send money to the Jewish National Fund for tree planting in Israel. Sometimes we plant a tree to honor a person we love or admire. But always, we are planting trees to help Israel grow and to make the land fruitful and beautiful.

TREES AND PEOPLE

Jews have often thought of trees as standing for life and strength. Sometimes they have compared people to trees. For instance:

A good person is like a cedar tree. The cedar grows straight, and so does a good person. The cedar's shade extends a great distance, and a good person's deeds help many others. The cedar reaches upwards, and a good person's heart reaches to God.

Can you make up your own saying about people and trees?

WORDS IN HEBREW

In Hebrew, letters stand for numbers, too. א is one, ב is two, and so on. The first word of the name for this holiday is really a number. ט is equal to 9; and ו is equal to 6. Add them up and you get the day of the month. The second word is the Hebrew month.

טו בִּשְׁבָט   TU bi-SHEVAT

And, Tu bi-Shevat has another name, too; one that tells us more about why we celebrate this day.

רֹאשׁ הַשָּׁנָה לָאִילָנוֹת   NEW YEAR OF THE TREES

Purim

The Great Rescue

The Purim story is full of adventure and suspense. It is in the Bible, in the Book of Esther.

Ahasuerus, the mighty king of Persia, gave a feast one night in his palace at Shushan. During the dinner he sent for his queen, Vashti. He wanted his guests to see how beautiful she was. But Vashti refused to come. This made the king very angry. He sent Vashti away and announced that he would choose a new queen to take her place.

THE NEW QUEEN

All the most beautiful girls in the kingdom were brought to Shushan: from these the king would choose his queen.

138

Now it happened that many Jews lived in Persia, and a lovely Jewish girl, Esther, was among those taken to see the king. Esther had been brought up by her uncle, Mordecai. Just before she was taken to the palace, Mordecai advised her, "Tell no one that you are Jewish."

Esther was gentle and beautiful, and King Ahasuerus fell in love with her. He set the royal crown upon her head and proclaimed her queen.

How Mordecai Saved the King

Now that Esther lived in the palace, Mordecai made it a habit to sit every day by the palace gate. In this way he could hear news of the palace and of the queen. That was how it happened that one day he heard two palace guards plotting to kill the king. Mordecai told Esther what he had heard; Esther told the king. The king ordered the guards to be seized and hanged, and it was written in the royal

THE KING CAN'T RULE

King Ahasuerus was not very good at thinking for himself. Most of his royal decisions were made by other people. For instance, when his first queen, Vashti, disobeyed him, Ahasuerus was angry but he did not know what to do. So he asked his advisors. They told him to send Vashti away and choose a new queen; and he took their advice.

When Haman told Ahasuerus that he wanted to kill the whole Jewish people, the king did not even want to be bothered thinking about it. He gave Haman permission to do whatever he wanted.

And when Ahasuerus wanted to honor Mordecai for saving his life, he could not think of any way to do it. So he asked Haman how it should be done.

It looks as though Ahasuerus was stupid, or lazy, or both.

Do you think that fact made it easier for an evil man to become prime minister? Why?

When Haman formed his plan to kill all the Jews in Persia, he was not expecting to do it all by himself. He was going to have the people living in the empire help him.

Once he had decided on the 13th of Adar, Haman sent a proclamation throughout the kingdom. He told the people that on that day they should attack the Jews and kill them all. Then the people could steal for themselves anything that had belonged to the Jews and keep it, said Haman.

Later, after Esther told King Ahasuerus about Haman's terrible plot, the king wanted to save the Jews. But there was no way to take back a royal proclamation. Instead, Mordecai and the king sent another proclamation, saying that on the 13th of Adar the Jews could fight back against anyone who attacked them. When the Persian people heard this news, many of them came over to the side of the Jews. And on the 13th of Adar the people who did attack the Jews, instead of destroying them, were destroyed by them.

That is why we celebrate Purim on the *14th* of Adar. The 13th was a day of struggle, but by the time it was over, the Jews had saved themselves. On the 14th of Adar they rested and celebrated their victory with "feasting and gladness."

book of chronicles that a Jew named Mordecai had saved the king's life.

HAMAN AND MORDECAI

Meanwhile, King Ahasuerus had promoted a man named Haman to the high post of prime minister. But Haman was an evil, spiteful man.

When Haman passed by, people everywhere were ordered to bow down to him. Mordecai, however, refused to bow down. This made Haman furious. He decided to take revenge not only on Mordecai, but on all of Mordecai's people: Haman would destroy all the Jews.

Haman went to the king and said, "There is a group of people in your kingdom who are different from everyone else. They do not keep the king's laws. It would be best for you to get rid of them. Give me permission to have them destroyed."

King Ahasuerus said, "I give you permission to do with these people whatever you think best." And he thought no more about it.

Then Haman cast lots (*pur*) as a way of deciding, by chance, on which day the Jews should be destroyed. He came up with the 13th of Adar. So the order was sent throughout the kingdom that on the 13th day of Adar the Jews would all be killed.

MORDECAI'S ADVICE

Jews everywhere—even Queen Esther—wept and mourned when they heard the news. Then Esther received a message from her uncle Mordecai: "Go to the king, and beg him to save the lives of your people." But Esther sent a message back to Mordecai, "This is the law: anyone who enters the king's court, without having first been called, will be put to death—unless the king holds out his golden scepter. I am afraid."

But Mordecai answered, "Don't think that you will be safer than all the other Jews, just because you live in the palace. And who knows? Perhaps you were made queen just so that you would be able to save your people in a time like this." Esther knew that Mordecai was right. She replied, "Ask all the Jews in Shushan to fast and pray three days for me. Then I will go to the king; and if I die, I die."

MORDECAI'S TRIUMPH *Haman is forced to honor Mordecai by leading him through the city, mounted on the king's horse. This etching is by the great artist Rembrandt.*

ESTHER'S PLAN

On the third day Esther put on her royal robes and went to the king's court. Ahasuerus, seated on his throne, looked up and saw his beautiful queen standing across the room. His heart was filled with love for her. He held out his golden scepter, and Esther drew near and touched the top of the scepter.

"What is your wish, Esther?" asked the king.

"Your majesty," replied Esther, "please come tomorrow to a dinner I have prepared for you, and let Haman, your minister, come, too." Gladly the king agreed.

Haman was thrilled to be invited to dine with the king and queen. But as he was leaving the palace, Haman saw Mordecai, who, as usual, did not bow down to him. This made Haman so angry that he decided not to wait for the 13th of Adar; he ordered a gallows to be built immediately, on which to hang Mordecai. "I will speak to the king about it in the morning," he said to himself.

THE KING HONORS MORDECAI

That night the king could not sleep. To pass the time, he asked his servant to read to him from the royal book of chronicles. When they came to the story of how Mordecai had saved the king's life, Ahasuerus asked, "What was done to honor Mordecai for this?" "Nothing at all, your majesty," the servant replied. Just then the king saw Haman waiting outside. "Come in, Haman," said the king, "and tell me: what should be done for a man whom the king wishes to honor?"

Haman proudly thought, "The king must wish to honor *me*." And so he said to Ahasuerus, "Let this man be dressed in the king's own clothes and mounted upon the king's own horse; and let one of the king's noble princes lead him on horseback throughout the city, announcing, 'This is the man whom the king delights to honor.' "

"A very good plan," replied the king. "It is Mordecai the Jew whom I wish to honor, and you shall lead him through the streets and make the announcement. Go quickly, and do it just as you described." Haman had no choice but to obey the king's command. He led the triumphant Mordecai through the city, and then went home, white with anger.

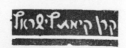

An old Purim badge showing Esther feasting with the king.

ESTHER'S FEAST

That evening the king and Haman came to dine with Esther. After they had feasted well, the king turned to Esther and said, "Now speak your request, for whatever you wish, I will grant it." Then said Esther, "O King Ahasuerus, my request is for my life, and the lives of my people—for we are all to be destroyed."

"Who dares to do this thing?" thundered the king. And Esther replied, "This wicked man, Haman."

The king was speechless with rage. But one of his servants spoke up, "Near Haman's house there stands a great gallows, on which he planned to hang Mordecai." Then Ahasuerus said, "Hang Haman on it." So they hanged Haman on his own gallows.

The Jews were saved. The king appointed Mordecai to be prime minister in place of Haman. And Mordecai proclaimed that the 14th of Adar would always be a day of feasting and merrymaking. Then Jews would never forget that they had lived to see their sorrow turned into joy, and their defeat into victory.

WORDS IN HEBREW

In ancient times books were written by hand on pieces of animal skin (parchment) or on paper made of reeds (papyrus). The sheets of paper or parchment were often sewed into a long scroll, which was rolled on a winder. Certain books of the Bible were made in this way, and they are still called "scrolls." The story you just read is called in Hebrew:

מְגִלַת אֶסְתֵּר   THE SCROLL OF ESTHER

144

Purim

Purim is the merriest Jewish holiday
of the entire year. On this day
children and adults alike are noisy,
jolly, even silly.

But, because the victory of Purim came very close to
being a defeat instead, some Jews observe a fast on the
day before Purim, the 13th of Adar. This is called the Fast
of Esther and reminds us that Esther and the Jews fasted
to prepare for Esther's all-important visit to the king.
Remembering the danger that threatened makes the
celebration that follows all the happier.

145

READING THE MEGILLAH

When the holiday arrives on the evening of Purim, the *Book of Esther* is read at the synagogue service. This book is called the *Megillah*, which means "scroll." The Megillah reading is different from any other synagogue reading in the year. It is like a big party. Instead of listening quietly, everyone in the congregation takes part in the reading. Whenever Mordecai or Esther is mentioned, we all cheer and whistle. But when the name of Haman is spoken we make such a racket—booing, stamping our feet, anything—that the noise totally drowns out the sound of that villain's name. Children are very good at this.

To help us make even more noise, we use noisemakers, called *gragers*. You can buy different kinds of gragers, or you can make one yourself. Then, when you hear the name of Haman, shake hard!

PURIM DAY

On Purim morning, the Megillah is read again in the synagogue, with the same noisy help. The rest of the day is for fun of all kinds. Children dress up in costume, pretending to be the characters in the Purim story. They parade around for everyone to see. Sometimes there is a contest, with prizes for the best costumes. But usually the Queen Esthers and Vashtis are all so beautiful, the King Ahasueruses all so royal, the Mordecais all so brave-looking, and the Hamans all so mean-looking, that picking a winner is very difficult.

On Purim, many congregations have parties or carnivals. Often there is entertainment—a Purim play (in Yid-

These Hasidic Jews from the Williamsburg section of Brooklyn, celebrate Purim by dressing in outlandish costumes.

Purim Fun

Playing music in an informal setting is one more way to enjoy Purim.

dish, a Purim *shpiel*), with plenty of silly jokes. In earlier times it was the custom to choose a Purim leader for the day, who could play jokes on everybody else. On Purim everyone eats the traditional food, *hamantaschen*, three-cornered cakes filled with fruit or poppy seeds. The name means "Haman's pockets," but the three-cornered shape is supposed to look like the hat Haman wore.

PURIM GIFTS

When Mordecai declared the holiday of Purim, he described it as a time "of feasting and gladness, and of sending food to one another, and gifts to the poor." Purim today is still a time for giving *shalah-manot*, gifts of food, to our friends and also to people who need them. In earlier times (and in some communities even today), children in costumes went from house to house, bringing gifts to everyone who lived in the town. Today, the Purim carnivals and plays often raise money for charity.

So Purim is a day for helping other people enjoy life while we enjoy it ourselves. A day for just plain fun. On Purim the air is filled with noise and laughter.

BE SILLY!

Traditionally, one of the ways to celebrate Purim is with a great feast, a banquet. In fact, Purim is the only day when, according to the Talmud, Jews are actually *supposed* to get drunk: adults drink until they cannot tell the difference between "Haman be cursed" and "Mordecai be blessed." In other words, Purim is a day when we let ourselves go; when we do not have to worry about the serious things of the world; when we can be as silly as we like.

All you need to make a grager is some kind of container that closes tightly and something to put inside the container that will rattle.

The container can be a small box, or a screw-top metal or plastic can. You can use a soft-drink can if you firmly tape up the opening. Or you can staple together two paper plates or paper bowls.

Before you close up your container, put inside it a few dried beans, dried corn kernels (popcorn), or pebbles.

For some kinds of gragers, you might want a handle. To make one, you can push the end of a stick between the edges of the two paper plates you are stapling together.

Decorate your grager with bright colors and designs or perhaps with the face of a character from the Purim story. You might want to glue on yarn for hair, or add other touches of your own.

Now you are ready to make Purim noise!

WORDS IN HEBREW

Hamantaschen and grager and shpiel are Yiddish words. The Yiddish language is a mixture of Hebrew and old German. For many hundreds of years, Jews who lived in the countries of northern Europe spoke Yiddish, so the words for ideas and things that became a part of Jewish life in those times are often in this language. However, ideas and things that are *very* old usually have Hebrew names. And ideas and things which are very new often have Hebrew names, too. Here is a very old idea—the idea that we should share our food on Purim. It comes from Mordecai himself. And here is a very *new* idea—the idea of calling hamantaschen (which, in Yiddish, means "Haman's Pockets") by a new name.

מִשְׁלוֹחַ מָנוֹת   GIFTS OF FOOD

אָזְנֵי הָמָן   HAMAN'S EARS

149

Purim

About Being
Mordecai and Esther

Purim gets its name from *pur*, the Persian word for "lot" (the kind of lot that you throw, like dice, in a game of chance); Purim means "lots." It is unbelievable, it is terribly evil, that anyone should be able to play with the lives of the Jewish people as if playing a game. In spite of the wonderful silliness of the Purim holiday, it is hard not to think a little about Purim's other, more serious side. We celebrate because our danger was turned to victory; but what a close call! What a danger it was!

Unfortunately, there have been many times in history

when Jews were threatened like this. In fact, even though the Book of Esther is very old, it clearly tells how anti-Semitism—which is another word for hatred of Jews—can spread and become dangerous.

How the Danger Grows

The hatred started small, with one man, Haman, who was wicked, jealous, and proud. But he was almost able to carry out his terrible plan to kill the Jews. That was because nobody else, not even the king, paid much attention—since they themselves were not threatened. It was also because Haman knew that people can be very greedy. He promised them that they would get rich by killing the Jews. And he made them feel suspicious of the Jews, saying that they were "different" from everyone else. That is how a huge country was brought almost to the point of killing all its Jews. No one spoke out in their favor. Only Jews themselves, led by Mordecai and Esther, came to their own defense.

After the proclamation which saved the Jews, many Persian people came over to the Jews' side. These people

---

"LITTLE PURIMS"

In certain places, Jews have had adventures so much like the Purim story that they are celebrated with a special "Purim." For example, hundreds of years ago in Spain, the king had a wicked adviser named Gonzalo who hated the Jews. Gonzalo told the king to drive all the Jews out of the country and seize the land and money that had belonged to them. The king agreed, and the Jews were about to be expelled. But a Jewish official, together with a Jewish woman whom the king loved, foiled this plot and saved the Jews.

MEGILLAH
A Purim megillah is a single scroll, often beautifully decorated. Did you ever hear the expression "a whole megillah"? The Megillah—the Scroll of Esther—is quite long. Sometimes people jokingly call any long story or explanation a "megillah."

did not hate the Jews; they admired their courage. But they could not be counted on to help the Jews while they were in danger.

THE MEANING OF PURIM TODAY

Many times during the history of the Jews, something like this has happened. People have turned their jealousy, fear, and anger against the Jews, and tried to destroy them. Not so long ago, in Nazi Germany, this brought about the Jews' greatest tragedy. The brave Mordecais and Esthers of that time were not strong enough to over-

LAUGHING IN THE FACE OF DANGER

Maybe this is the most amazing thing about Purim: out of the threat of being destroyed came a very happy, high-spirited holiday. Perhaps the Jews would not have been able to live through so many dangerous times if they had not been able to laugh—even to laugh at themselves and at their miseries. On Purim we laugh and make merry because it is good to laugh. If your life is difficult, as it was for Jews celebrating Purim in many earlier times, it is also good to laugh. We laugh because long ago in Persia the Jews turned things upside down. They changed the day of their destruction into the day of their great victory. And we laugh because we are glad to be celebrating a happy holiday together with Jews everywhere, remembering the long-ago history that we all share, and the loyalty that still binds us together.

come their powerful enemy. Now in our own time, the Jewish State of Israel works hard to defend itself against enemies who want to see it destroyed.

From the Book of Esther we see how important it is for Jews to be loyal to each other. Even though the ways we live may be very different, we all belong, in a way, to one great family. If there are Jews in trouble somewhere, they need our help; and some day we may need theirs. Esther came to the aid of her people, even though it meant risking her own life. Today Jews all over the world help and support the Jews of Israel—because they are in danger—and the Jews of Russia—because they are not free. If we come to the aid of our own people, even when it is hard to do, we will win out over whatever dangers may threaten us. We have always needed, and we will always need, Mordecais and Esthers.

WORDS IN HEBREW?

The name of this holiday comes from a *Persian* word. Persian was the language of the people who conquered Babylonia. And Babylonia was a land in which many of our people lived for hundreds of years. Most of the Persian rulers were friendly to the Jews; even Ahasuerus was not unfriendly—he was just foolish enough to fall for Haman's evil plan. And it was Haman who cast lots (which is like throwing dice) to decide the day the Jews would die. So, when the Jews won out, they called their new holiday by a name which would remind them of what happened:

פּוּרִים PURIM ("LOTS")

153

An old drawing of Queen Esther.

Lag ba–Omer

The Picnic Holiday

Do you remember what the Omer is? It is the bundle of barley that was brought to the Temple in early days. On the second day of Passover, an omer was offered to God, in thanks for the harvest; then 49 days were counted as the season of the Omer. On the 50th day came the holiday of Shavuot.

Lag ba–Omer is a short way of saying "The 33rd day of the counting of the Omer." (*Lag* is made up of the letter *lamed*, , which is used for the number 30, and the letter *gimel*, , used for the number 3. Together these two letters stand for the number 33.) The time of counting the 50

154

days of the Omer is a quiet, serious time. The ancient Israelites, who were mostly farmers, watched their crops anxiously during this time, worrying and waiting. By the 50th day of the Omer, the second crop, wheat, would be ripe. If the crop grew well during this time there would be plenty of grain, but if not, hunger and hardship might follow. So the 50 days of counting were days of tension. During that time there were no joyous activities, no weddings or feasts.

But the 33rd day of the Omer is an exception. It became, in later days, a time of happy celebration, one day of weddings and playfulness in the middle of those quiet times.

LAG BA-OMER IN ROMAN TIMES

Lag ba–Omer became a holiday in the days after the destruction of the Second Temple: after Judea had been conquered by the Roman armies, and forced to live under Roman law. The rule of the Romans was cruel, especially where religion was concerned. Jews were forbidden to study or to teach the Torah. But there were great Jewish teachers at that time who refused to bend to Roman rule. One of them, Simeon ben Yohai, continued to study Torah despite the law against it. Finally he had to flee from the Romans to save his life. He escaped to the wild hills of Galilee and lived in a cave there, with his young son. For 13 years Simeon and his son hid in the cave, living on wild fruits and water from a spring.

Rabbi Simeon's students could no longer study Torah with their teacher. But they did not forget their great master. Every year, on the 33rd day of the Omer, they came into the hills to see Simeon, and to listen once again to his stirring words.

Because the cave in which Simeon hid with his son was near the northern city of Meron, many Jews still gather at Mount Meron on Lag ba–Omer, to honor Simeon. Some say he died on Lag ba-Omer, another reason for honoring him on this day.

A second rabbi who refused to obey the Roman law was Rabbi Akiva. Akiva saw how clever the Roman emperor was. If Jews stopped studying the Torah as the emperor commanded, they would soon forget why being Jewish was so important. They would be like the other peoples who had been conquered by the Romans, had become like the Romans, and finally had disappeared—never to be heard of again.

Akiva continued to teach his students the lessons of Torah. But finally he was warned that the Romans were

THE LEGEND OF RABBI AKIVA

Legends have grown up about the 33rd day of the Omer. One of them is about Rabbi Akiva. The rule of Rome was so cruel that secret plans were made to revolt and fight for freedom. The brave Bar Kokhba was the leader of this Jewish revolt. Rabbi Akiva went up and down the country asking people to follow Bar Kokhba, and many of Akiva's thousands of students became soldiers as well as scholars. The Jews fought long and bravely, but in the end the mighty Roman army was too powerful for them, and the revolt failed.

In the days of fighting, a strange, terrible disease appeared. Many of Rabbi Akiva's students died from it. But on the 33rd day of the Omer, very suddenly, the disease stopped spreading and disappeared. So Lag ba-Omer became, for another reason, a day for rejoicing in the midst of sadness.

Lag ba-Omer is often celebrated with picnics and bonfires.

looking for him. So Akiva made a plan. He told his students to carry bows and arrows and picnic lunches and to go out into the fields as if they were going hunting. When the Roman soldiers saw the Jews going out "to hunt," they let them pass. But each day when the Jews reached the fields, Akiva met them and taught them Torah! Whenever they saw the Roman soldiers approaching, the students pretended to be hunting or playing games.

CELEBRATING LAG BA–OMER

In later centuries Lag ba–Omer became a holiday for schoolchildren: instead of spending the day in school, the whole class went picnicking in the woods, taking toy bows and arrows to play with. And today we, too, have a school picnic on Lag ba–Omer.

Lag ba–Omer is not a major Jewish holiday. But it has been, over the centuries, a day for Jews to remember some of our wisest heroes and to celebrate with joy. In some places people dance around great bonfires and feast on this day. And because it is about students, Lag ba–Omer has always been a special day for schoolchildren: so special that it was once the day when the younger children could boss the older ones, who had to do as they were told! Lag ba–Omer belongs to students—it is *your* day.

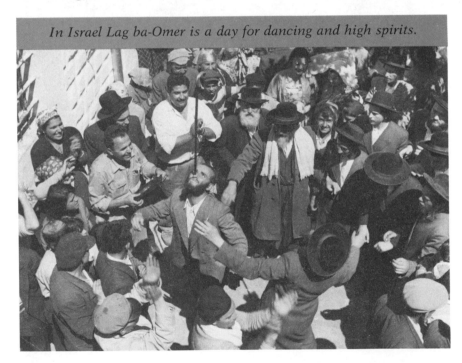

In Israel Lag ba-Omer is a day for dancing and high spirits.

Among the very Orthodox, a three-year-old son is given his first haircut on Lag ba-Omer, and a party is held to celebrate the event.

WORDS IN HEBREW

Lag ba-Omer is another holiday name made up of a number and a word. The number is 33 (ל equals 30; and ג equals 3), and the word is our old friend the Omer, the 49 days that we count between Pesah and Shavuot.

ל״ג בָּעֹמֶר   THE 33RD DAY OF THE OMER.

Tisha be-Av

Remembering Sorrows

There have been Jews for thousands of years. In the course of that long time there have been many happy events to celebrate, but also some evil ones to remember. Since biblical days there has been a special day for mourning these tragedies. It is called Tisha be-Av, the ninth day of the month of Av, and it comes during the summer.

160

Remembering the First Temple

On the ninth of Av, or on days very near to it, a number of terrible things happened to us. Several thousand years ago, in 586 B.C.E., the first great Temple in Jerusalem was destroyed. That beautiful Temple had been built by King Solomon to be a permanent home for the Ark of the Torah. It was the central Temple for all of ancient Israel: it was the center of the Jewish religion and the symbol of God's covenant with the Jewish people.

Solomon's Temple stood for over 400 years. But then the land was invaded and conquered by armies from the huge, powerful land of Babylonia. The Babylonian king, Nebuchadnezzar, ordered his armies to bring thousands of Israelites back to Babylon. There the Jews had to live, as captives, far from their own home. Nebuchadnezzar also had riches brought to him from Israel, including the precious objects from the Temple; and the Temple itself was burned to the ground.

Those were terrible days for the Israelites. No longer were they free people, living in their own land. Their Temple had been invaded and destroyed; they themselves were forced to live as strangers in a strange land. The book of the Bible called Lamentations is made up of sad poems about our fallen nation:

> How the city sits an outcast
> That once was filled with people!
> She has become a widow,
> She that was great among the nations.
> A princess among the other lands,
> Now she has become a slave . . .
> She has no one to comfort her.

This is a model of the city of Jerusalem as it appeared in 70 C.E., just before the destruction of the Second Temple. In the center is the Temple, seen from the front.

The Second Temple

The Western Wall is all that remains of the Second Temple. Thousands of worshippers pray there every holiday.

In time, Jews returned to Jerusalem. They rebuilt the Temple. Israel again became a busy, growing land. But it was often ruled by some huge empire—Persian, Greek, or Roman. Sometimes that rule was gentle, but the Romans were so cruel that at last the Jews rebelled. The tiny nation fought back against the powerful Roman Empire, so bravely that it took four years for the Romans to defeat them. When the Roman armies did finally capture Jerusalem, they looted the sanctuary and set fire to the second Temple. This happened on the ninth day of Av, in the year 70 c.e.

The Romans were determined to destroy the Jewish state, to be sure that there could never be another rebellion. So they dealt very cruelly with the Israelites. There

THE SECOND TEMPLE—YOU CAN STILL SEE IT

After the first destruction, the Jews who returned to Israel rebuilt the Temple according to the plan of Solomon's Temple, although not as grandly. Many additions were made to it over the years. It was this second Temple that the Maccabees rescued and rededicated.

During the Roman times, the Temple was rebuilt and greatly enlarged by King Herod. When the Romans seized Jerusalem and burned the Temple, one part of the outer wall survived and still stands today. The great Western Wall has been a very important symbol for Jews ever since the Temple's destruction 2,000 years ago. The Western Wall is a symbol of Israel's earlier glory. Jews came to this wall to weep for the destruction of the Temple and the scattering of the Jewish people. That is why it was often called the "Wailing Wall." At the wall they prayed, hoping the Jews would one day be able to come back to Israel again. Today the Western Wall is in the modern State of Israel, where you can visit it. It is a place for prayer, for remembering our long, long past, and for feeling hopeful about our future. Where once we wept, today we feel proud.

were some Jews living in other lands, where life was not so hard. Little by little, Jews in Israel began to move to these lands. But, Israel was still their center and homeland.

THE DIASPORA

In the centuries that followed, Jews gradually scattered out from Israel more and more, to all the lands around the Mediterranean Sea and far beyond. This spreading out is called the *Diaspora*, the Greek word for "scattering." For close to two thousand years, Jews have lived in the Diaspora, as we do now.

We can see, then, what a serious, important thing happened when the second Temple was destroyed, on the ninth of Av so many years ago. It changed everything for us. We no longer had a land of our own: we became scattered through all the countries of the world.

On Tisha be-Av we mourn the destruction of the two Temples and other terrible times that have come upon our people. It is a day of sadness. But it also contains hope. Over the centuries, many other peoples and religions have disappeared altogether, after being conquered or scat-

SHOWING WE ARE SAD

On Tishah be-Av we can show our sadness by fasting. We fast to help us feel a little of the suffering our ancestors felt. In the synagogue, we read the Book of Lamentations.

Tishah be-Av is a day of mourning. Just as if someone in the family has died, traditional Jews on this day do not bathe or carry on their usual activities. In the synagogue the lights are dimmed, the Ark is draped in black, and the people sit on low boxes.

You can read in the Bible a very detailed description of how the first Temple was built. Solomon ordered fine cedar trees to be cut in the mountains of Lebanon; the huge logs were floated in the Mediterranean Sea, down the coast to Israel. Enormous stones were carefully cut before they were brought to the site of the Temple. The Temple was a long rectangle, "60 cubits long, 20 cubits wide and 30 cubits high" (a cubit is about 1½ feet long). It was divided into three rooms: first, a porch; second, a main room; and last the Holy of Holies, a small room in the heart of the Temple in which the Ark was placed. The Temple was built of stone. Its roof and its inside walls were of cedar, carved all over with designs of flowers and palm trees. Many parts were overlaid with gold. There were two brass columns in the porch, a huge brass fountain, and an altar, candlesticks, lamps, and other objects all of gold. All in all, it took Solomon seven years to build this beautiful "house to the Name of the Lord."

(If you want to read about it for yourself, look in the Bible in the First Book of Kings, chapters five and six.)

tered. But the Jewish people live. So on this day, although our hearts ache for the suffering that Jews have been through, we know that we are strong, and will go on.

WORDS IN HEBREW

Like Tu bi-Shevat, this holiday takes its name from the date on which we celebrate it, the ninth day of the Hebrew month of Av. Unlike Tu bi-Shevat, this is one of our saddest days, a day of fasting. On this day we remember the destruction of the ancient Temples in Jerusalem. Both the first and the second Temples had the same Hebrew name. Here are some Hebrew words for Tisha be-Av:

תִּשְׁעָה בְּאָב	THE NINTH OF AV
יוֹם צוֹם	DAY OF FASTING
בֵּית הַמִּקְדָּשׁ	HOUSE OF HOLINESS (THE TEMPLE)

165

Modern Holidays

Some holidays are new—ten, or twenty, or fifty years old. Just as Jews did thousands of years ago, we make a new holiday when something happens that changes our lives. Some of our new holidays are sad; some are happy and triumphant. But all of them have the same purpose: to remind us of the things that are too important to forget.

Yom Hashoah

Day of the
Holocaust

Holidays help us remember our history as Jews. Many things that happened to us were great and wonderful—like the victory of the Maccabees; we remember them with celebration. But some events have been horrible, heartbreaking. We remember them with special days, too: even sad lessons must not be forgotten.

Yom Hashoah means "day of the whirlwind." This is the day set aside for remembering the most terrible disaster that ever befell the Jews. This day of remembrance is very new. Your grandparents probably remember the grim events that it stands for.

These events are often called "the Holocaust." A holocaust is a complete burning up, a total destruction. It is the Jews who were burned up and destroyed in this holocaust.

Although Jews had lived in the countries of Europe for hundreds of years, many of their neighbors still disliked them and thought of them as inferior or as troublemakers. In Germany, a man came to power in 1933 who truly hated the Jews. His name was Adolf Hitler. He had plans of tremendous evil: to make Germany ruler of the whole world, and to get rid of all the Jews everywhere. Hitler blamed all of Germany's problems on the Jews. He promised the German people that without the Jews they would become masters of the world. Many millions of people believed him. Many others were afraid to speak up, because they thought Hitler would destroy them, too.

Hitler's German Nazi army invaded a number of countries and conquered most of them. Meanwhile, his police forced Jews throughout Europe to live in special, fenced-off areas, called ghettos; and then, to go into huge, overcrowded prisons, out in the country where no one else

THE WARSAW GHETTO UPRISING

The most famous Jewish resistance, one of many, took place in Warsaw, the capital of Poland. There the poorly armed Jews fought back bravely, inside their ghetto, against powerful Nazi troops. They held out for nearly a month, until finally the ghetto was overrun. But even after that, fighters hid out around Warsaw and continued to battle against the Nazis. The date of Yom Hashoah, the 27th of Nisan, is close to the day on which the Warsaw ghetto uprising began, to help us remember that brave battle.

Jewish prisoners in the concentration camp at Buchenwald.

Faces of the Holocaust

A Jewish family has been captured by Nazi soldiers in the Warsaw Ghetto.

Many countries have built monuments to honor those who died in the concentration camps. This memorial is in Paris.

could see them. These were called concentration camps. In the concentration camps some Jews were made to work as slaves, and the rest—thousands, millions of Jews— were killed. They were shot, or killed with poison gas, or starved to death.

Many Jews did not realize that they were going to be killed. They could not believe that such a terrible thing was going on. Others, who found out what was happening, tried to fight back against Hitler's forces. (They were helped by a small number of non-Jews.) These Jewish fighters were very brave, but they could not stop Hitler's huge army, with its tanks, airplanes, and machine guns.

WORLD WAR II

While Hitler was murdering the Jews, his German army was waging war against half the world. The Nazis were very powerful, but in the end the United States, along with England and other allies, defeated the German army and destroyed Hitler.

After many battles, World War II was finally over. The few Jews who were still alive in concentration camps were freed. Many of them went to live in Israel, or the United States. But an unbelievably large number—*six million* men, women, children, and babies—had been

YOM HASHOAH CUSTOMS

Many synagogues hold special prayer services on Yom Hashoah. Often, memorial candles are lit in memory of the six million of our people who died. On Yom Hashoah Jews everywhere say the *Kaddish*, the mourner's prayer, with special meaning.

killed. There were practically no Jews left in the whole eastern part of Europe. Whole neighborhoods, schools, towns, stood empty. About one-third of all the Jews had been murdered.

When the world learned what Hitler and his Nazis had done, people everywhere were filled with horror. They understood that the Holocaust was the most terrible thing that human beings have ever done to other human beings.

A Day For Remembering

On Yom Hashoah we remember the Holocaust. We remind ourselves that sometimes people can be unbelievably evil to other people. We remind ourselves that too often it is the Jews against whom their hatred is turned. We cry in our hearts for the countless good, ordinary people who were murdered just because they were Jews.

We know that this is only part of the story. We know that people can be good as well as evil. We know that many people fought bravely, and that some non-Jews gave up their lives to save Jews.

We do not feel hopeless. Even though what happened was more horrible than anyone could have imagined, we Jews go on. Many Jews who lost their homes in Europe have a new home now, in the Jewish State of Israel. Many live in lands of freedom, such as England, Canada, Australia, and the United States. We will never forget the Holocaust. But remembering it will help make us strong: so that the Jews will hope, and grow, and live.

The Holocaust makes us think of the Book of Esther. Hitler was like Haman who long ago was filled with hatred and wanted to kill all the Jews. Just as in ancient Persia, other people were too selfish or too cowardly to try to stop such a terrible plan. But this time there was no brave Jewish queen like Esther, no one powerful enough to turn defeat into victory. The Jews were not saved from their enemies. The horrible plan was carried out.

WORDS IN HEBREW

In English we speak of the Holocaust. A holocaust can be a great destruction, but it also has the meaning of a sacrifice. In Hebrew, the Holocaust is called a whirlwind, as if it were a tornado or hurricane with such great force that it destroyed everything it touched. The name expresses both the great sadness we feel and the chilling fearfulness of the event:

שׁוֹאָה THE WHIRLWIND (HOLOCAUST)

We call this day:

יוֹם הַשׁוֹאָה THE DAY OF (REMEMBERING) THE WHIRLWIND

Yom Ha'atzma'ut

**Israel's
Birthday**

Yom Ha'atzma'ut is Israel's Independence Day, the birthday of the young State of Israel. Like the birthday of anyone we love, it is a happy, festive day; we are very glad that Israel was reborn.

We know about the ancient, biblical land of Israel, the land God promised to the Jews. We know that after Israel was conquered and the second Temple burned, Jews were forced to scatter among the other countries of the world. There no longer was a Jewish state; it had been destroyed. And the Jews lived in foreign lands for almost 2,000 years.

Then, only a little while ago, the amazing new State

174

of Israel came into being. Modern Israel is so young that your grandparents remember when it did not exist at all.

How did the new Israel begin?

ISRAEL THROUGH THE AGES

After biblical Israel was destroyed, a small number of Jews remained in the land. For hundreds of years the land belonged to one huge empire or another. Most Jews lived in other countries, where they learned the languages and customs of their new homes. But often Jews were mistreated. Many things were not allowed, for them. Sometimes even their lives were in danger.

Although hundreds and hundreds of years passed, the Jews did not forget their ancient land. They no longer spoke Hebrew except in the synagogue, but they still studied it. Each year at the Passover Seder they said, "Next year in Jerusalem."

NEW SETTLERS IN AN ANCIENT LAND

About one hundred years ago, a small group of Jews living in Russia decided to settle in the land of Israel, which was

THE HEBREW MIRACLE

One of the most amazing things the early pioneers did was to bring an ancient language back to life. Hebrew had not been an everyday, spoken language for almost *2,000* years. But from the start, the settlers wanted Hebrew to be the language of their new land. They built schools where everyone studied Hebrew, and gradually, as children were born and grew up, Hebrew became a natural spoken language. Many new words had to be invented, to talk about all the parts of our lives that did not exist in biblical times—like bicycles and telephones!

PIONEERS *These early pioneers arrived in Palestine in 1880 and began one of the very first settlements. They are eating dinner in the rocky fields they worked to farm.*

Zionism

ARRIVAL *These Jews survived the Holocaust and in 1946, at long last, arrived in Israel.*

then called Palestine. When they got there, they found a place that was mostly desert. The orchards and farms of the biblical "land of milk and honey" had gone to ruin centuries ago. The people living in Palestine (there were both Jews and Arabs) were poor, and did not know how to farm or build in modern ways.

The new settlers seemed to face an impossible job. It was very hot. There was not enough water. There were dangerous tropical diseases. But the pioneers (ḥalutzim) kept on. They worked incredibly hard. They started farms; they irrigated and fertilized the dry desert land, and soon they were able to grow fruits and vegetables. They set up schools and began to build towns.

MODERN ZIONISM

Meanwhile, in Europe, a young Jewish writer named Theodor Herzl decided that it was very important for the Jews to have a country of their own, just as all other people have. This belief is called Zionism. Herzl wrote books about Zionism and worked to spread his ideas to other people. The idea of rebuilding the Jewish homeland

PEOPLE AND THINGS

Zionism is the belief that the Jews should have a country of their own, a homeland, in Israel. If you believe in helping Israel, then you are a *Zionist*.

Theodor Herzl was the founder of modern Zionism. He gave all his energy working for his dream of a Jewish State in Israel. Herzl spoke with the leaders of many governments to win their support for a Jewish state.

Chaim Weizmann led the Zionist movement after Herzl, and became the first president of the new State of Israel.

David Ben-Gurion, another great Zionist, was the first prime minister of the new State of Israel.

1948 is the year in which Israel became a nation.

began to catch on. More Jews left their homes in Europe to help build a new land in Palestine.

But Palestine still did not belong to the Jews. It belonged to the Turkish Empire. In World War I, the Turks were defeated and Palestine was placed under British protection. The British promised that the Jews would be able to establish their own country in Palestine, but they also made promises to the Arabs who lived in Palestine.

Meanwhile, Hitler rose to power in Germany and World War II began. By the time that war was over there was a new, very important reason for setting up a Jewish homeland: those thousands of Jews who had somehow survived the Holocaust now had no place to go. They needed a home, some place where they could start a new life.

Finally in 1947 the United Nations decided to establish two countries, a Jewish one and an Arab one, side by side in little Palestine. On May 15, 1948, the State of Israel was born.

ISRAEL'S WAR OF INDEPENDENCE

But on the very next day, armies from five different Arab countries all attacked Israel. The Jews had been willing to settle for half of Palestine, but the Arabs were not. They wanted to drive out the Jews completely.

Israel had a tiny army. She had very little ammunition, no large cannons, no tanks, only a few tiny planes. The Arab invaders had tanks, cannons, and many more soldiers. They thought winning would be easy.

They were wrong. Israel's soldiers fought with fierce

Arabs attacking Jerusalem Jews.

bravery. After many months of fighting, the Arab armies were beaten, and they agreed to end the fighting.

ISRAEL TODAY

Israel is still surrounded by enemies, who have waged new wars against it many times. In spite of that, tiny Israel has done astonishing things. Not so long ago, it was a land of deserts and swamps. Now it is filled with modern cities, hospitals, museums, schools, and factories. Many Jews, from all over the world, have found a new home there.

Israel is a kind of miracle. Two thousand years ago it was destroyed; one hundred years ago it was just an idea: now it lives! No wonder we celebrate Israel Independence Day with great joy. In Israel, and in Jewish communities around the world, there are happy parades. We wave the Israeli flag and feel proud on this day, proud of Israel—so tiny, so brave, so old, and so young.

ISRAEL IS SPECIAL

Tiny Israel is surrounded by many large countries. But she is the only free country among them. In that whole part of the world (the Middle East), Israel is the only democracy—the only land where all the people can vote and direct the government, instead of being ruled *by* the government.

Judaism is part of the Israeli way of life. Jewish holidays are the national holidays of Israel. Stores close on Shabbat; people dance in the streets on Simḥat Torah; and on the High Holy Days, the sound of the shofar is heard far and wide. In Israel, Jews are truly free to be themselves, to practice Judaism, and to live full Jewish lives.

For Jews outside of Israel, this new nation is like a second home. Jews everywhere look to Israel with pride, for at long last our people have returned to our ancient homeland.

WORDS IN HEBREW

Israel is the land in which Hebrew came back to life. Here are some words in Hebrew that help us remember what we celebrate on Israel's birthday.

יוֹם הָעַצְמָאוּת	DAY OF INDEPENDENCE
צִיּוֹן	ZION (THE LAND OF ISRAEL)
צִיּוֹנוּת	ZIONISM
יִשְׂרָאֵל	ISRAEL

180

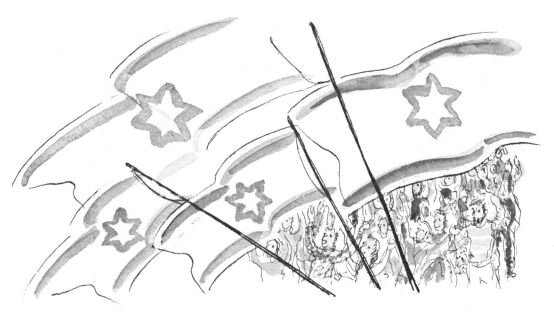

Yom Yerushalayim
and Yom Hazikkaron

Days of Joy
and Honor

In 1948 the modern State of Israel was born. Immediately all the surrounding Arab countries attacked Israel. There followed a hard, bloody war—Israel's war of independence.

YOM YERUSHALAYIM

In Jerusalem the fighting was heavy. The Israeli fighters had pitifully few guns and very little other equipment. The Arabs were able to surround the old Jewish section of the city and cut it off from the rest of Israel. There was no way for the Israelis in that area to receive shipments of food or ammunition. Finally the Arabs succeeded in capturing the old Jewish section.

When the fighting between Israel and the Arabs ended at last, and a cease-fire line was drawn between the two sides, the line went right through Jerusalem. The western side of Jerusalem was on the Israeli side. The eastern section, the oldest part of the city, was in the hands of the Arabs.

So Jerusalem, which has been our holy city for thousands of years, became a divided city. A barbed-wire fence cut through it, guarded by armed soldiers.

On the Jewish side, Arabs were permitted to live as they always had and to worship in their mosques. But on the Arab side, the synagogues were burned. Worst of all, the Jews were cut off from their holiest place. In Jerusalem's Old Jewish Quarter is the Temple Mount, where thousands of years ago the Temple stood. The ancient Temple wall, the "Western Wall," was now in Arab territory. There was no way that Jews could visit and pray at this holy place.

OUR JERUSALEM

Jerusalem has been our center ever since King David proclaimed it to be the capital of ancient Israel, about 3,000 years ago. Solomon built the Temple here. But after the destruction of ancient Israel and the scattering of Jews all over the world, Jerusalem was ruled by foreign nations for many hundreds of years. Now, at last, the Temple Mount and the ancient Temple wall stand once again in a Jerusalem that is the capital of a Jewish nation—just as in the days of the Bible.

JERUSALEM DAY   *Israeli soldiers, both men and women, march through the streets of Jerusalem to celebrate Yom Yerushalayim.*

Half of Jerusalem had been torn away. And Israel lived uneasily alongside the Arab countries, suffering occasional fighting and bloodshed for years.

Nineteen years later, in 1967, the Arabs once again launched an attack on Israel. Again little Israel fought alone against the armies of many Arab countries. Israel's soldiers were well-trained and very brave. Not only did they fight the Arabs off: they pushed on and captured much Arab territory. Their counterattack was so strong that the entire war was over in six days! It is known as the Six Day War.

Most important of all, in this war the Jews recaptured the old section of Jerusalem. Now the two parts of Jerusalem could be rejoined, and the city could be whole again. Hundreds of thousands of Jews traveled to Jerusalem to pray at the ancient Western Wall; many wept tears of joy.

Yom Yerushalayim means "Jerusalem Day." It is our new holiday, celebrated on the 28th of Iyar, on which we express our great joy that Jerusalem is united once again.

183

YOM HAZIKKARON

Yom Hazikkaron means "Remembrance Day." It is a memorial day, for remembering all the brave soldiers who died fighting for Israel—in the War of Independence, and in other wars that followed, such as the Six Day War.

Yom Hazikkaron is celebrated in Israel on the day before Yom Ha'atzma'ut (Independence Day). It is a solemn day. Many soldiers gave their lives; if they had not, there would be no Israeli independence to celebrate with joy and pride.

On Yom Hazikkaron the Israeli flag is flown at half-mast, and memorial candles are lit in synagogues, schools, army camps, and public places. Ceremonies are held at the military cemeteries, to honor the soldiers who are buried there; honor guards of Israeli soldiers stand at attention.

In the morning, sirens blow all across the country, followed by two minutes of complete silence. Throughout Israel, everything stops—traffic, machinery, talk, all activity. Israelis remember, then, that they owe their freedom to the courage of those who have fought and died. In their minds and hearts, they honor these soldiers, and pray for them.

When evening comes, and the first stars appear, a long siren blast is heard. Remembrance Day, Yom Hazikkaron, is over; Israel Independence Day, Yom Ha'atzma'ut, has begun.

The Israeli memorial day is Yom Hazikkaron. Each year, on this day in late April, Israelis remember and honor those who died in battle. Many people visit a military cemetery to mourn the soldiers, relatives, friends, or strangers, who fell defending Israel.

SO MUCH TO REMEMBER

In the United States we have Memorial Day, on which we honor all the brave soldiers who have died fighting for the United States. Although the United States has fought in many wars, for a long time no war has actually been fought on our land, or has threatened our homes. It is sometimes hard for us to realize what it means for people to fight, and die, so that their families and fellow citizens can live in freedom. But in Israel, war is very close to home. There was fighting only a short time ago, and there may be more fighting soon. Every family has someone in the army—an aunt, a brother, a cousin. On Remembrance Day in Israel, everyone understands how much is owed to Israel's soldiers; and everyone honors their brave spirit; and everyone remembers.

WORDS IN HEBREW

These are the names for the two holidays you have just studied:

יוֹם יְרוּשָׁלַיִם   JERUSALEM DAY

יוֹם הַזִּכָּרוֹן   REMEMBRANCE DAY

185

Rosh Ḥodesh

The Jewish Calendar We Jews have our own special way of counting time. Think, for example, of a day. According to the calendar we use in daily life, day begins at midnight and ends the following midnight. But a Jewish day begins at sundown and ends the following sundown. We get this idea directly from the Bible. In the very beginning, God separated the light from the darkness: "And there was evening and there was morning, the first day."

The Jewish calendar is different, too. The calendar generally used in the modern world is a sun calendar. It measures a year by the number of days it takes for the

186

earth to revolve around the sun (365¼). That year is divided into months.

COUNTING BY THE MOON

But the Jewish calendar began with the moon. From early times, Jews counted days by the new moon. The new moon is a very thin crescent moon. Each night the crescent appears larger, until one night the moon is full; then in following nights the moon begins to look smaller. Finally it disappears altogether. And, on the following night, the new moon, the thin crescent, appears again.

Jewish months follow the moon. It is 29½ days from one new moon to the next, so Jewish months are usually 29 or 30 days.

ROSH HODESH

In ancient days, Jews watched the evening sky to keep track of the days. When a new moon was seen, the day was proclaimed *Rosh Hodesh*, the "head of the month." Rosh Hodesh is a holiday; in earlier days it was a kind of small Rosh Hashanah, a new beginning. Special prayers are said on this day. And several evenings after the new moon's appearance, observant Jews gather outdoors to thank God: "Blessed are You, Lord our God . . . Who has told the moon to renew itself. . . ."

THE MOON AND THE SUN

The Jewish calendar does not count by the moon alone; it combines moon-counting with sun-counting to keep track of time. That is because it takes about 12½ cycles of

WHY HOLIDAYS MAY BE CELEBRATED FOR TWO DAYS

In Bible times, when the new moon was seen in Jerusalem, a new month—Rosh Ḥodesh—was proclaimed. Then messengers were sent all over Israel to announce the new month. But it took longer for the news to reach Jews living outside of Israel. They worried that they might be starting their months on the wrong day, and therefore celebrating holidays on the wrong day, too. So they began to celebrate each major holiday for an extra day, just be be sure. Outside of Israel, Shavuot lasts for two days instead of one, and Passover for eight days instead of seven.

Even though for many centuries we have been sure our calendar is correct, traditional Jews living outside Israel still celebrate the major holidays for another day.

the moon to make one cycle of our earth around the sun, one seasonal year. If we just used a calendar of 12 moon months, we would soon get out of rhythm with the seasons. We would be celebrating Passover in the winter, and Ḥanukkah in the autumn.

So we have leap years. On each leap year we add not just a day (like February 29th), but a whole extra month. Every two or three years we have a leap year. (That is why Jewish holidays seem to jump around a little in relation to the regular calendar.) This system keeps the moon months and the sun years in rhythm together.

THE JEWISH YEAR

We Jews have our own kind of day and our own calendar. The time of the Jewish new year is different, too. Actually, we have more than one new year. According to the Torah, the year begins in the spring, with the month of Nisan. This is not only the time when life begins each year, but is also the month in which we were freed from Egypt. That makes it the time that we began to be free people—our "beginning."

MOON AND EARTH *These photographs were taken from the spacecraft Apollo. Visible in this view of the Earth are most of Africa and parts of Europe and Asia, including Israel.*